THE WORKBOOK ON THE
Christian Walk

THE WORKBOOK ON THE
Christian Walk

Maxie Dunnam

UPPER
ROOM BOOKS

All scripture quotations not otherwise identified are from the *Revised Standard Version* of the Bible, copyright ©1946, 1952, 1971 by the Division of Christian Education of the National Council of Churches in the USA. Used by permission.

Scripture quotations designated TEV are from the *Good News Bible, The Bible In Today's English,* copyright © by American Bible Society 1966, 1971, 1976, and are used by permission.

Scripture quotations designated NRSV are from the *New Revised Standard Version,* copyright ©1989 by the Division of Christian Education of the National Council of Churches of Christ in the United States of America, and are used by permission.

Scripture quotations designated PHILLIPS are from *The New Testament in Modern English,* copyright ©1958 J.B. Phillips. Used by permission of The MacMillan Company.

Scripture quotations designated NEB are from *The New English Bible.* ©The Delegates of Oxford University Press and The Syndics of the Cambridge University Press 1961, 1970. Reprinted with permission.

Any scripture designated AP is the author's paraphrase.

Excerpt from "Healthy Conflict" by Donald J. Shelby. Used by permission.

Excerpt from "We are Not Alone" by James W. Moore. Used by permission.

Excerpt from "You're Better than You Think" by Mark Trotter. Used by permission.

Excerpts from "Star Performer" by J. Ellsworth Kalas. Used by permission.

Excerpts from letters on pages 47-48 are used by permission of Von Davis.

Excerpt from letter on page 63 is used by permission of Lissa Noel.

Excerpts on page 83 are used by permission of Mary Levack.

Excerpt from "Who Is Responsible for that Empty Chair?" by William M. Schwein. Used by permission.

Excerpt from "Declaration to Demonstration" by Rodney E. Wilmoth. Used by permission .

Excerpt from "Prisoners of Hope" by Joe C. Pool. Used by permission.

Excerpt from letter on page 131 is used by permission of Timothy J. Forbess.

"The Warrior Is a Child" by Twila Paris copyright (c) 1984 Singspiration Music/ASCAP. All rights Reserved. Used by permission of The Benson Co., Inc., Nashville, TN.

While every effort has been made to secure permission, we may have failed in a few cases to trace or contact the copyright holder. We apologize for any inadvertent oversight or error.

Cover design: John Robinson
Printed in the United States of America
First printing: December, 1991 (20)
Second printing: January, 1993 (20)
ISBN 0-8358-0640-5

To Jerry—
whose walk with me in marriage
has sustained, shaped, and cheered
my Christian Walk.

CONTENTS

Introduction to The Christian Walk

WE HAVE BEEN SEDUCED BY THE NOTION that anything worthwhile can be acquired at once. If anything can be done, we falsely conclude, it can be done quickly and efficiently. The thirty-second TV commercial and *The Reader's Digest* abridgement mentality have shortened our attention span. The microwave oven and instant coffee symbolize a culture that has no patience for, little understanding of, and minimal appreciation for discipline and long-term commitment.

Christians do not escape the pressure of the Instamatic world in which they live. Thus there is an alarming lack of follow-through on Christian experience. Persons make honest decisions for Christ but their journey to Christian maturity is cut short. Why?

The mind-set of the world offers no support for the journey. In Christian discipleship there are no shortcuts, no time or distance-saving detours. The tourist mind-set that has captured religion in our time will not do. Christian discipleship is not about religious entertainment, or enjoyable visits to particular places of worship, or the latest expressions of Zen or faith-healing or psychology or contemporary worship (whatever that means). It is, to use a phrase from Frederick Nietzsche, a "long *obedience* in the same direction."

Eugene H. Peterson wrote a book on discipleship in an instant society for which he used Nietzsche's phrase as a title: *A Long Obedience in the Same Direction.* In it, he said:

> In going against the stream of the world's ways, there are two Biblical designations for people of faith that are extremely useful: *disciple* and *pilgrim*. *Disciple (mathetes)* says we are people who spend our lives apprenticed to our master, Jesus Christ. We are in a growing-learning relationship, always. A disciple is a learner, but not in the academic setting of a schoolroom, rather at the work site of a craftsman. We do not acquire information about God, but skills in faith.
>
> *Pilgrim (parepidemos)* tells us we are people who spend our lives going someplace, going to God, and whose path for getting there is the way, Jesus

Christ. We realize that "this world is not my home" and set out for the "Father's House" (Peterson, p. 13).

Discipleship and pilgrimage are what this workbook is all about. Our metaphor is the Christian Walk. It is a dominant image in the New Testament. Jesus, the Gospel writers, and Paul all employed the image, especially Paul. Jesus called himself "the way" (John 14:5), and the first Christians were called "followers of the way." The writer of the Epistle to the Hebrews gave us a succinct guide for the dynamic process of Christian discipleship:

> Wherefore, seeing we also are compassed about with so great a cloud of witnesses, let us lay aside every weight, and the sin which doth so easily beset *us,* and let us run with patience the race that is set before us, looking unto Jesus the author and finisher of our faith; who for the joy that was set before him endured the cross, despising the shame, and is set down at the right hand of the throne of God.   —Hebrews 12: 1-2, *KJV*

He uses the word run but he adds the phrase *with patience*. It is the same image: Run with patience—walk.

No theme lends itself more to a workbook approach than the Christian Walk. It is not something we simply read about; it is something we practice. So this workbook will provide content to read and grapple with cognitively. But more importantly, it will call us to effective involvement and an exercise of the will—to be and to do as well as to know.

Do you remember Dick Rutan and Jeana Yeager? They were the pilots who completed a globe-circling, non-stop airplane flight without refueling. People said it couldn't be done, but they did it. More than 50,000 people greeted them at Edwards Air Force Base when they returned from flying some 26,000 miles without refueling. They faced some anxious moments when an electrical pump failed, the one that is used to draw fuel from the tank. Jeana also suffered from bruises when unexpected turbulence tossed her into the cabin wall and ceiling. But they made it ahead of schedule.

Mobil Corporation provided the synthetic oil for what they described as the toughest test in aviation history. The company bought a full-page ad in *USA Today* congratulating Yeager and Rutan and promoting their product. The ad closed with these words: "We believed it could be done, but you, Dick and Jeana, proved it. And doing beats talking every time."

Until we are willing to act, our words are not going to mean very much. People would rather see what we do than hear what we say.

Let's look at the process of this workbook. It is simple, but very important.

The Plan

I have found in my long years of teaching and ministry with small groups that a six to eight week period for a group study is the most manageable and effective. Also, I have learned that persons can best appropriate content and truth in "small doses." That is the reason for organizing the material in segments to be read daily.

The plan for this workbook is the same as for the previous ones I have written. It calls for a seven-week commitment. You are asked to give thirty minutes each day to learn about and appropriate ideas and disciplines for your Christian Walk. For most persons, the thirty minutes will come at the beginning of the day. However, if it is not possible for you to give the time at the beginning of the day, do it whenever the time is available, but do it regularly. The purpose of this spiritual journey must not be forgotten: to incorporate the content into your daily life.

It is an individual journey, but my hope is that you will share it with some fellow pilgrims who will meet together once each week during the seven weeks of the study.

The workbook is arranged into seven major divisions, each designed to guide you for one week. These divisions contain seven sections, one for each day of the week. Each day of the week will have three major aspects: reading about the discipline, reflecting and recording ideas and thoughts about the material and your own journey, and, finally, some practical suggestions for incorporating ideas from the reading material into your daily life.

In each day's section, you will read something about the Christian Walk. It won't be too much to read but it will be enough to link you with the challenges of your Christian Walk—problems, experiences, relationships and situations with which we must cope. Included in the reading will be some portions of scripture, the basic resource for Christian discipline and living. Quotations from most sources other than scripture are followed by the author's name and page number on which the quote can be found. These citations are keyed to the *Notes* section at the back of the workbook where you will find a complete bibliography should you wish to read certain works more fully.

Throughout the workbook you will see this symbol * * *. When you come to the symbol, *please stop*. Do not read any further. Think and reflect as you are requested to do in order to internalize the ideas being shared or the experience reflected upon.

Reflecting and Recording

After the reading each day, there will be a time for reflecting and recording. This dimension calls you to record some of your reflections. The degree of meaning you receive from this workbook is largely dependent upon your faithfulness to its practice. You may be unable on a particular day to do precisely what is requested. If so, then simply record that fact and make a note of why you can't follow through. This may give you some insight about yourself and help you to grow.

Also, on some days there may be more suggestions than you can deal with in the time you have. Do what is most meaningful for you, and do not feel guilty.

The emphasis in this workbook is upon growth, not perfection. Don't feel guilty if you do not follow exactly the pattern of the days. Follow the content and direction seriously, but not slavishly.

Finally, always remember that this is a personal pilgrimage. What you write in your personal workbook is your private property. You may not wish to share it with anyone. For this reason, no two people should attempt to share the same workbook. The importance of what you write is not what it may mean to someone else, but what it means to you. Writing, even if it is only brief notes or single-word reminders, helps us clarify our feelings and thinking.

The significance of the reflecting and recording dimension will grow as you move along. Even beyond the seven weeks, you will find meaning in looking back to what you wrote on a particular day in response to a particular situation.

Sharing with Others

In the history of Christian piety, the spiritual director or guide has been a significant person. To varying degrees, most of us have had spiritual directors—persons to whom we have turned for support and direction in our spiritual pilgrimage. There is a sense in which this workbook can be a spiritual guide, for you can use it as a private venture without participating in a group.

Its meaning will be enhanced, however, if you share the adventure with eight to twelve others. In this way, the priesthood of all believers will come alive, and you will profit from the growing insights of others, and they will profit from yours.

John Wesley believed that "Christian conferencing" was a means of grace for Christians. By Christian conferencing he simply meant Christians sharing intentionally their Christian experience and understanding in deliberate and serious conversation. He designed the "class meeting" as a vehicle for this discipline. In such a fellowship of Christian conversation and shared life, "one loving heart sets another on fire." Your weekly gathering can be that kind of means of grace. A guide for group sharing is included in the text at the end of each week.

If this is a group venture, all persons should begin their personal involvement with the workbook on the same day, so that when you come together to share as a group, you all will have been dealing with the same material and will be at the same place in the text. It will be helpful if you have an initial get-acquainted group meeting to begin the adventure. A guide for this meeting is provided in this introduction.

Group sessions for this workbook are designed to last one and one-half hours (with the exception of the initial meeting). Those sharing in the group should covenant to attend all sessions unless an emergency prevents attendance. There will be seven weekly sessions in addition to this first get-acquainted time.

A group consisting of eight to twelve members is about the right size. Larger numbers will tend to limit individual involvement.

One person may provide the leadership for the entire seven weeks, or leaders may be assigned from week to week. The leader's task is to:

1. Read the directions and determine ahead of time how to handle the session. It may not be possible to use all the suggestions for sharing and praying together. Feel free to select those you think will be most meaningful and those for which you have adequate time.
2. Model a style of openness, honesty, and warmth. A leader should not ask others to share what he or she is not willing to share. Usually the leader should be the first to share, especially as it relates to personal experiences.
3. Moderate the discussion.
4. Encourage reluctant members to participate and try to prevent a few persons from doing all the talking.
5. Keep the sharing centered in personal experience, rather than academic debate.
6. Honor the time schedule. If it appears necessary to go longer than one and one-half hours, the leader should get consensus for continuing another twenty or thirty minutes.
6. See that the meeting time and place are known by all, especially if meetings are held in different homes.
7. Make sure that the necessary materials for meetings are available and that the meeting room is arranged ahead of time.

It is a good idea for weekly meetings be held in the homes of the participants. (Hosts or hostesses should make sure there are as few interruptions as possible from children, telephone, pets, and so forth.) If the meetings are held in a church, they should be in an informal setting. Participants are asked to dress casually, to be comfortable and relaxed.

If refreshments are served, they should come *after* the formal meeting. In this way, those who wish to stay longer for informal discussion may do so, while those who need to keep to the specific time schedule will be free to leave, but will get the full value of the meeting time.

Suggestions for Initial Get-Acquainted Meeting

Since the initial meeting is for the purpose of getting acquainted and beginning the shared pilgrimage, here is a way to get started.

1. Have each person in the group give his or her full name and the name by which each wishes to be called. Do away with titles. Address all persons by their first name or nickname. If name tags are needed, provide them. Each person should make a list of the names somewhere in his or her workbook.

2. Let each person in the group share one of the happiest, most exciting, or most meaningful experiences he or she has had during the past three or four weeks. After everyone has shared in this way, let the entire group sing "The Doxology"or a chorus of praise.

3. After this experience of happy sharing, ask each person who will to share his or her expectations of this workbook study. Why did he or she become a part of it? What does each expect to gain from it? What are the reservations?

4. The leader should now review the introduction to the workbook and ask if there are questions about directions and procedures. (The leader should have read the introduction prior to the meeting.) If persons have not received copies of the workbook, the books should be handed out now. Remember that every person must have his or her own workbook.

5. **DAY ONE** in the workbook is the day following this initial meeting, and the next meeting should be held on **DAY SEVEN** of the first week. If the group must choose a weekly meeting time other than seven days from this initial session, the reading assignment should be adjusted so that the weekly meetings are always on **DAY SEVEN,** and **DAY ONE** is always the day following a weekly meeting.

6. Nothing binds group members together more than praying for one another. The leader should encourage each participant to write the names of each person in the group in his or her workbook, and commit to praying for them by name daily during the seven weeks.

7. After checking to see that everyone knows the time and place of the next meeting, the leader should close with a prayer, thanking God for each person in the group, for the opportunity for growth, and for the possibility of growing through spiritual disciplines.

One final note: If someone in the group has an instant camera, ask him or her to bring it to the group meeting the next week. Be prepared to take a picture of each person in the group to be used as an aid to prayer.

A Word of Gratitude

Scores of persons have shared my Christian Walk in special ways, but none so intimately as my wife Jerry. Her understanding and unconditional love have not only shaped my Christian Walk, but have made possible an impossible schedule that enables me to write books, using time that rightfully belongs to her. As much as anyone I know, she demonstrates a generosity of self that is characteristic of the Christian Walk. My public thanks to you.

And my special thanks to Mary K. Marino, my administrative assistant, who types my sermon manuscripts for every Sunday, and who has gone above and beyond the call of duty in word processing the manuscript for this book.

WEEK ONE

Look Carefully How You Walk

———

DAY ONE
The Main Thing

BUMPER STICKERS ARE EFFECTIVE MEANS OF COMMUNICATION. I don't put them on my car, but I'm happy other people do. Not only do they provide a pleasant diversion when you are driving in busy traffic; sometimes their messages provide profound wisdom, practical guidance, or just a good laugh.

The same is true for the little signs and cartoons and posters that people put up on bulletin boards. That these sayings posted on bumper stickers and bulletin boards are effective is proven by the fact that they get your attention and that often you remember for a long time what they say. That's what communication is all about.

I think I will never forget this one: THE MAIN THING IS TO KEEP THE MAIN THING THE MAIN THING. I thought of it again as I began preparation of this workbook. The main thing for Christians is what we call discipleship— being a learner and follower of Jesus. The metaphor I am using for that dynamic life is the Christian Walk.

The call of Jesus to his first disciples was the call "follow me."

As he walked by the Sea of Galilee, he saw two brothers, Simon, who is called Peter, and Andrew his brother, casting a net into the sea—for they were fishermen. And he said to them, "Follow me, and I will make you fish for people." Immediately they left their nets and followed him. As he went from there, he saw two other brothers, James son of Zebedee and his brother John, in the boat with their father Zebedee, mending their nets, and he called them. Immediately they left the boat and their father, and followed him.

—Matthew 4:18-22, NRSV

Jesus went out again beside the sea; the whole crowd gathered around him, and he taught them. As he was walking along, he saw Levi son of Alphaeus sitting at the tax booth, and he said to him, "Follow me." And he got up and followed him.

—Mark 2:13-14, NRSV

But these are not the only instances in which the specific call to "follow me" is used. When Jesus wanted to define the meaning of discipleship, he expressed it very clearly. "If any man would come after me, let him deny himself and pick up his cross and follow me" (Matthew 16:24).

And you remember the story of the rich young ruler who asked Jesus, "What shall I do to inherit eternal life?" Jesus told him to keep all the commandments, and he responded that he had kept all the commandments. Then Jesus observed, "One thing you still lack. Sell all that you have and distribute to the poor, and you will have treasure in heaven; and come, follow me" (Luke 18:22).

On another occasion, he put the demands of discipleship in this fashion: "He who loves his life loses it, and he who hates his life in this world will keep it for eternal life. If anyone serves me, he must follow me; and where I am, there shall my servant be also . . . ." (John 12:25-26).

And do you remember that beautiful claim of Jesus to be the Good Shepherd? He says that the shepherd goes before his sheep and the sheep follow him, for they know his voice. And then he adds these words, "A stranger they will not follow . . . ." (John 10:5).

The call of Christ for us to follow him is a call for us to walk in his path, to walk in his way.

Reflecting and Recording

Spend a few minutes thinking about Christ's initial call to you. Can you recall the occasions or the time frames in your life when it was clear that Christ was calling you to follow him? Write a few sentences describing the occasions or time frames, your feelings, the circumstances, your age, the setting or settings in which the call came.

During the Day

Flash prayers are momentary thoughts and expressions sent heavenward on random occasions during the day. It is helpful to have everyday happenings—the ringing of the phone, a knock at the door, stopping for a traffic light, settling into a chair to wait for an appointment, waiting in the check-out line at the store, going to the mailbox—call you and remind you to offer such prayers. Today, let some of these common happenings signal you to offer this flash prayer: "Lord Jesus, thank you for calling me."

DAY TWO
"Walk, walk . . . ."

For we are his workmanship, created in Christ Jesus unto good works, which God hath before ordained that we should walk in them.   —Ephesians 2:10, *KJV*

I therefore, the prisoner of the Lord, beseech you that ye walk worthy of the vocation wherewith ye are called . . . .   —Ephesians 4:1, *KJV*

This I say therefore, and testify in the Lord, that ye henceforth walk not as other Gentiles walk, in the vanity of their mind . . . .   —Ephesians 4:17, *KJV*

Be ye therefore followers of God, as dear children; And walk in love, as Christ also hath loved us, and hath given himself for us an offering and a sacrifice to God for a sweet-smelling savour.   —Ephesians 5:1-2, *KJV*

For ye were sometime darkness, but now *are ye* light in the Lord: walk as children of light . . . .   —Ephesians 5:8, *KJV*

Wherefore he saith, Awake thou that sleepest, and arise from the dead, and Christ shall give thee light. See then that ye walk circumspectly, not as fools, but as wise, redeeming the time, because the days are evil.
                                   —Ephesians 5:14-16, *KJV*

"WALK" WAS A FAVORITE IMAGE OF PAUL. The above six references are from Ephesians alone. But it is not only in Ephesians that the image appears over and over again; you find it in his other letters as well.

That ye might walk worthy of the Lord . . . .   —Colossians 1:10, *KJV*

We were buried therefore with Him by baptism into death, so that as Christ was raised from the dead by the glory of the Father, we too might walk in newness of life.   —Romans 6:4

Let us walk honestly, as in the day . . . .   —Romans 13:13, *KJV*

So we are always of good courage; we know that while we are home in the body we are away from the Lord, for we walk by faith, not by sight.

—2 Corinthians 5:6-7

We could go on and on, and we will be focusing on these texts throughout this workbook. The image is there, one of the clearest images in the New Testament: the Christian Walk.

But it is not only to be found in the New Testament. One of the statements used to describe great persons of faith in the Old Testament was this: He or she walked with the Lord. It was beautifully expressed in describing Enoch. Could there be a more telling epitaph? "And Enoch walked with God: and he *was* not for God took him" (Genesis 5:24, *KJV*).

Bishop Edward Tullis tells of arriving early for a worship service at a church where he was to preach. They were having the closing exercises in Sunday School. A nine-year-old girl had the role of telling the story of Enoch. Probably with some help from her parents, she had written the story in her own words and she told it flawlessly. She closed with this beautiful line: "Enoch was such a close friend of God that one day they took a long walk together, and Enoch never came back."

Isn't that beautiful? And isn't it a powerful image? Walking with the Lord. The Christian Walk.

Reflecting and Recording

Yesterday, I invited you to recall and reflect on Christ's initial call to you. Think now about your Christian life. Can you recall an occasion in the past few months when Christ called you to walk in some special way—maybe in relation to someone, or to perform a particular task, or to take on a special responsibility? Describe that experience.

During the Day

Continue using the flash prayer: "Lord Jesus, thank you for calling me."

DAY THREE

Nothing Static about the Christian Life

Not that I have already obtained this or have already reached the goal; but I press on to make it my own, because Christ Jesus has made me his own. Beloved, I do not consider that I have made it my own; but this one thing I do: forgetting what lies behind and straining forward to what lies ahead, I press on toward the goal for the prize of the heavenly call of God in Christ Jesus. Let those of us then who are mature be of the same mind; and if you think differently about anything, this too God will reveal to you. Only let us hold fast to what we have attained.   —Philippians 3:12-16, *NRSV*

THE IMAGE OF THE CHRISTIAN WALK SUGGESTS SOMETHING DYNAMIC. There is movement to it—a growth, an energy, a vitality. There is nothing static about the Christian life.

Some time ago, I came across this shocking word in John Wesley's *Journal*:

My friends affirm I am mad, because I said I was not a Christian a year ago. I affirm I am not a Christian now . . . . For a Christian is one who has . . . love, peace, joy. But these I have not . . . . though I have given, and do give, all my goods to feed the poor, I am not a Christian. Though I have endured hardship, though I have in all things denied myself and taken up my cross, I am not a Christian. My works are nothing . . . . I have not the fruits of the Spirit of Christ. Though I have constantly used all the means of grace for twenty years, I am not a Christian (Wesley, vol. 2, pp. 125-126).

Do you know when John Wesley wrote that? It was eight months after Aldersgate. And you know what happened at Aldersgate. It was there, after years of endless struggle, that John Wesley came to the point of what we would call justification by grace through faith, or the assurance of salvation. And do you remember his testimony? "I felt my heart strangely warmed. I felt I did trust in Christ, Christ alone for salvation; and an assurance was given me that He had taken away *my* sins, even *mine,* and saved *me* from the law of sin and death" (Wesley, vol. 1, p. 476).

So what is going on here? It is only eight months after the experience that moved him to his very core and brought forth that lilting testimony. What is going on here? Wesley is emphatic. "I am not a Christian!" How do we read that—the extreme way Mr. Wesley makes the case, and the way he uses the word, Christian? The big issue that we must not miss is the point of his turmoil. He's wrestling with himself, and agonizing as Paul did in his Epistle to the Romans.

> For I know that nothing good dwells within me, that is, in my flesh. I can will what is right, but I cannot do it.   —Romans 7:18

There is no question about it—Wesley was a Christian. Yet, he was not a Christian.

"Hold on," I can hear you say. "Stop the double talk. How can you say Wesley was a Christian and he was not a Christian. What sort of talk is that?" I understand that you would think it's double-talk. And I know why your question might be insistent. Can Wesley be a Christian and not a Christian at the same time?

Well, it's not double talk. In his *Journal*, Wesley was pouring out his soul. He was anguishing in his relationship to God. I am certain he could say with Paul, "Christ Jesus has made me his own." But, also like Paul, Wesley would make no claim to have attained the fullness of what he knew was his by gift and promise.

And that must be our stance. That is the Christian stance. To be aware of what is yet lacking in our being perfected and to press on "grasping even more firmly that purpose for which Christ Jesus grasped me" (Philippians 3:12, *PHILLIPS*). The Christian's life is never static.

I think we need to learn a lesson from shrimp. You know they wear their skeletons on the outside of their bodies. They've been known to discard their shells as many as 26 times during a lifetime. They shed their shells to accommodate their growing bodies.

We need to be like that, confessing with Paul that we know we have not arrived spiritually, but we press on. We continue to grow; for the Christian, life is never static.

Reflecting and Recording

For most of us, the Christian life, our discipleship, is an up-and-down affair. We know the intimacy of walking with Jesus, but we also know the experience of the disciple who followed Jesus from afar. Let the following time line represent the past three years of your life. Put a date at the beginning, three years ago, and the present date at the end.

•------------------------•------------------------•------------------------•

The second mark represents 2 years ago. Put a date there. The third mark represents one year ago. Put a date there.

Now plot your Christian growth, graph-like, through this three year period—the highs and the lows, as to how closely you were walking with Christ, how vividly you knew his presence, or how distant he seemed. Do that now.

Make some notes about what was happening at the high, low, and level points of your graph.

During the Day

Change your flash prayer for today. Make it a petition: "Lord Jesus, help me to follow you closely today."

DAY FOUR

Look Carefully Then How You Walk

> For once you were darkness, but now you are light in the Lord; walk as children of light (for the fruit of light is found in all that is good and right and true), and try to learn what is pleasing to the Lord. Take no part in the unfruitful works of darkness, but instead expose them. For it is a shame even to speak of the things that they do in secret; but when anything is exposed by the light it becomes visible, for anything that becomes visible is light. Therefore it is said, "Awake, O sleeper, and arise from the dead, and Christ shall give you light." Look carefully then how you walk, not as unwise men but as wise, making the most of the time, because the days are evil. Therefore do not be foolish, but understand what the will of the Lord is.   —Ephesians 5:8-17

IF THE CHRISTIAN LIFE IS NEVER STATIC, we must be careful how we walk. That was Paul's specific word to the Ephesians—"look carefully then how you walk" (v. 15).

Let me ask you a question. If you get to where you are going, will you be where you want to be? You can chew on that one all week, and I hope you will. If you get to where you are going, will you be where you want to be?

I once heard a statement that described the plight of too many of us. "There are people who use up their entire lives making money so that they can enjoy the lives they have entirely used up." Another person put it this way: "What some people mistake for the high cost of living is really the cost of high living."

We need to be careful how we walk before we get to where we are going and discover it's not the place we wanted to be.

One big truth we must reckon with as we consider our walk is that there is a spiritual thirst in our life that will never be satisfied apart from a growing relationship with God. The psalmist spoke for us all, "As a hart longs for flowing streams, so longs my soul for thee, O God" (Psalm 42:1). The King James Version translates it "as the hart panteth after the water brooks."

Now we may not know it. We may think we are driven by something other than a thirst for God—the need for success, for achievement, for sex, for recognition, or for money. We may not even think that we are particularly religious, not in comparison with those around us who seem to really be preoccupied with the faith. We may think that we are always concerning ourselves with mundane things and not even thinking much about God. But that's not the way it is at all. Even though we may not recognize it, there is a spiritual thirst in our lives that will never be satisfied apart from a growing relationship with God.

Do you remember Paul's encounter with the Athenians? Athens was one of the world's intellectual centers, the site of a great university. Innumerable religious cults seemed to be attracted to the city. Paul was preaching in the synagogues and he aroused a lot of attention, especially the attention of the philosophers on Mars Hill. So they invited Paul to the Areopagus to address them.

Paul was brilliant in his speech. He had observed thousands of statues and idols that dominated that ancient city, so he began his sermon with the word, "Men of Athens, I perceive that in every way you are very religious." He continued:

> For as I passed along and observed the objects of your worship, I found also an altar with this inscription, "To an unknown god." What therefore you worship as unknown, this I proclaim to you. The God who made the world and everything in it, being Lord of heaven and earth, does not live in shrines made by man, nor is he served by human hands, as though he needed anything, since he himself gives to all men life and breath and everything.   —Acts 17:23-25

Paul was right. God created us in such a way that we would always seek him. St. Augustine captured the truth of it: "For Thou has made us for Thyself and our hearts are restless till they rest in Thee." We seek to satisfy that thirst in a lot of different ways. Most of us believe that it's a matter of finding the right style—doing the right thing at the right time in the right manner, living in the right place and knowing the right people, belonging to the right clubs and buying the right wine and going to the right restaurants, choosing the right job or profession. Sometimes we even include going to the right church.

Isn't that the appeal of the whole advertising industry? The ad world preaches a gospel that life is found by acquiring style. They make style the religion that satisfies. Notice the sacrifices that people are willing to make in order to acquire style. And have you ever thought that that really is the test of religion? In fact, what you are willing to sacrifice for determines what your religion is.

That is what our friend was saying, "There are people who use up their entire lives making money so that they can enjoy the lives they've entirely used up."

It simply doesn't work. So we need to keep on asking ourselves the question: If we get to where we are going, will we be where we want to be? And we need to remember the admonition: *Look carefully then how you walk.*

Reflecting and Recording

Go back to **DAY TWO** and read again the verses from Paul, setting forth the Walk as the metaphor for Christian discipleship. Select the one that speaks most convincingly to you. Spend a few minutes reflecting on it, then offer a prayer in response to it.

During the Day

Today, at those times when you have been praying a flash prayer, ask yourself the question, "If I get to where I am going, will I be where I want to be?" After mulling that over for a minute, add your flash prayer: "Lord Jesus, help me to follow you closely today."

DAY FIVE

The Nuclear Truth of New Testament Christianity

You were dead through the trespasses and sins in which you once lived, following the course of this world, following the ruler of the power of the air, the spirit that is now at work among those who are disobedient. All of us once lived among them in the passions of our flesh, following the desires of flesh and senses, and we were by nature children of wrath, like everyone else. But God, who is rich in mercy, out of the great love with which he loved us even when we were dead through our trespasses, made us alive together with Christ—by grace you have been saved—and raised us up with him and seated us with him in the heavenly places in Christ Jesus, so that in the ages to come he might show the immeasurable riches of his grace in kindness toward us in Christ Jesus. For by grace you have been saved through faith, and this is not your own doing; it is the gift of God—not the result of works, so that no one may boast. For we are what he has made us, created in Christ Jesus for good works, which God prepared beforehand to be our way of life.

—Ephesians 2:1-10, *NRSV*

AMOS ALONZO STAGG WAS ONE OF THE GREAT FOOTBALL COACHES of all time. As a coach, he constantly tried to keep his substitutes prepared and ready on the bench. He had the habit of prompting alertness by suddenly popping questions at them while the game was underway.

One afternoon he turned to a fourth-string player who hadn't been in a game a single minute during the whole season. Stagg barked, "You, Cartmell! What would you do if we had possession of the ball with one minute to play, the score tied, and we had only four yards to go for a touchdown."

"Well, Coach," the young man stammered, "I probably would slide down to the end of the bench so I could see better."

Paul was a lot like Coach Stagg. He always tried to keep his listeners and readers alert, ready to play the game, and equipped for the Christian Walk.

In the magnificent passage of Paul to the Ephesians that is recorded above, Paul is almost singing the Gospel. He is moving along in a musical cadence when, in verse 5, he puts a parenthesis. "By grace you have been saved." Then he returns to his theme, only to come back again in verses 8, 9, and 10 to complete what he had introduced in verse 5. What he stated there in verses 8, 9, and 10 is what John MacKay has called the "nuclear truth of New Testament Christianity."

> For by grace you have been saved through faith, and this is not your own doing; it is the gift of God—not the result of works, so that no one may boast. For we are what he has made us, created in Christ Jesus for good works, which God prepared beforehand to be our way of life.   —Ephesians 2:8-10, NRSV

By grace you have been saved is the ringing conviction of Paul's life. Verses 8 through 10 of Ephesians are really a summary of the first five chapters of Paul's letter to the Romans. It was Paul's bold and radical belief that we can do nothing to earn the favor of God; we only receive through faith what he has given us. His salvation is grace—all grace.

This expression of the nuclear truth of New Testament Christianity is enriched by its setting here in the Ephesian letter. It is in this letter that Paul's theology is set to music. Edgar J. Goodspeed, the eminent New Testament scholar, refers to chapters one and two of Ephesians as "a *Jubilate* over the blessedness of the Christian salvation" (Goodspeed, p. 20).

Look at how the second chapter begins as recorded in the Revised Standard version: "And you he made alive." That is a *Jubilate,* isn't it? "And you he made alive, when you were dead through the trespasses and sins in which you once walked . . . " (Ephesians 2:1-2).

You could tell me your story (I hope you could tell it), and I would love to hear it. Nothing moves my soul more, nothing quickens me to new life and new resolve to be dependent upon God's grace, than to hear someone tell about how they were made alive by Christ Jesus.

We used to sing a song down in Eastside Baptist Church in Perry County, Mississippi, and sometimes we would sing it beneath the brush arbors the men would build for a revival meeting led by an itinerant preacher who didn't have a church. I do not remember all of the song, but a part of it went like this, though I am not sure now that these were the precise words:

> I can tell you now the time; I can take you to the place,
> Where the Lord saved me by his wonderful grace.
> But I cannot tell you how, and I cannot tell you why,
> But I will tell you all about it in the bye and bye.

Even if we can or can't tell the time and the place (and many of us can't, and that's okay), we certainly can't tell how or why because it's all grace, and grace is a mystery. But what we know, if we know what we need to know about the Christian gospel, is that "(we) he made alive when (we) were dead in the trespasses and sins in which we once walked."

Reflecting and Recording

On **DAY ONE**, you were asked to recall and reflect upon your experience of Christ's initial call to you to follow him. Get in touch with that experience.

If I asked you, When did you first accept Christ as your Savior? or When were you first aware of the fact that *by grace you have been saved through faith; and this is not your own doing, it is the gift of God?* would you recall and name the same experience of hearing Christ's initial call to follow him?

Reflect for a few minutes. Are the experiences the same? If not, how are they connected? How different?

***

During the Day

Continue your flash prayer exercise, asking first, "If I get to where I am going, will I be where I want to be?" Then pray, "Lord Jesus, help me to follow you closely today."

DAY SIX

You He Made Alive

You were dead through the trespasses and sins in which you once lived, following the course of this world, following the ruler of the power of the air, the spirit that is now at work among those who are disobedient.

—Ephesians 2:1-2, *NRSV*

THE PREDICAMENT AND THE POSSIBILITY OF EACH OF US is here in these words. The predicament: You were dead through the trespasses and sins in which you once walked. The possibility: You he made alive.

Sin equals death, and God's answer to death is resurrection. That resurrection is a present reality. You he made alive. Let's stay with these realities. First, the predicament.

Does it prick your mind like a sharp thorn, these stark images: "following the course of this world, following the ruler of the power of the air, the spirit that is now at work among those who are disobedient."

Is that too stark for reality? Not at all.

At 12:21 a.m., on a morning in November, 1979, a doctor pronounced Jesse Walter Bishop dead in a gas chamber of the Nevada State Prison. Bishop was a career criminal who committed his first armed robbery at the age of fifteen, and spent twenty-two of his last twenty-seven years behind bars. Bishop renounced all efforts to stay his execution for a murder he had committed in 1977. At that time he even waived his right to a jury trial, immediately pleading guilty. He could have been given an appeal of his case even minutes before entering the gas chamber, but he refused it with these words: "This is just one more step down the road of life that I've been heading all my life. Let's go."

One agonizes about such a life and shudders at such a steel-encased set of the will. But we can also learn.

Sin is not to be played with, not to be taken casually, not to be looked at tentatively as though we can do as we please, order our lives as we will, change when and if we wish, thinking we will always be in control. There is a cumulative effect that builds, until our hearts may be petrified and we are past feeling. We really see the horror of that possibility: that sin may kill our wills, and we may thus be doomed to a walk that can only end in death.

The predicament is horrible and clear: *dead in trespasses and sin.*

But think of the possibility: to be made alive in Christ.

Christians are those who have already been made alive. The resurrection after death to eternal life promised in the New Testament is the heritage only of those who have already been made alive through Christ in their earthly existence. We may not like to think of it, but the Bible is clear: The end toward which everything moves is God's judgment. In the ninth chapter of Hebrews, it says, "It is appointed unto men once to die, and after this the judgment . . . ." (vs. 27, *KJV*). And in John's Gospel, Jesus makes the case especially clear: "Do not marvel at this; for the hour is coming when all who are in the tombs will hear his voice and come forth, those who have done good, to the resurrection of life, and those have done evil, to the resurrection of judgment" (John 5:28-29).

The astounding and liberating truth is that we share in Christ's resurrection now. Christ so identified himself with us in his life and death that his death was a representative and inclusive event. He died for us. His resurrection is therefore inclusive as well. To be with Christ and in Christ is to share his new life now.

And it is in the midst of that resounding proclamation of our predicament and possibility that Paul interrupts himself to give us an expression of the nuclear truth of New Testament Christianity: "For by grace you have been saved through faith; and this is not your own doing, it is the gift of God."

Reflecting and Recording

In two or three words, ("I believe it," "It can't be true," "Never happen," or "I wish it were so with me,") write your spontaneous response to these statements:

And you he made alive.

_____

Sin can kill our wills, and we may be doomed to a walk that can only end in death.

_____

It is appointed unto man once to die, and after this the judgment.

_____

To be with Christ and in Christ is to share his new life now.

_____

Do you know someone who is still dead in trespasses and sins? Pray for that person. Also pray that you will have the opportunity soon to share your being-made-alive-by-Christ experience with that person.

During the Day

Change your flash prayer to something like this: "Thank you, Christ, for your forgiveness, and for making me alive."

DAY SEVEN

By Grace Through Faith

> But God, who is rich in mercy, out of the great love with which he loved us even when we were dead through our trespasses, made us alive together with Christ—by grace you have been saved . . . .   —Ephesians 2:4-5, *NRSV*

HERE IS A PICTURE OF THE EXTRAVAGANT LOVE OF THE DIVINE FATHER, bending down over his dead children and loving and cherishing them, always. We can do a lot, in fact we all do a lot, to separate ourselves from God. We exercise our selfishness, our self-will, our sensuality; we give ourselves to all forms of sin; and all of that is within our capacity and freedom to do. But there is one thing we can't do. We can't prevent God loving us.

Do you remember that rather pathetic picture of David in the Old Testament? He has heard of the death of his darling son, Absalom. He's oblivious to the fact that Absalom has turned against him and become a rebel. He remembers only that this was his boy. So he bursts into that painful and monotonous wail that, over the centuries, has been the deepest expression of undying fatherly love. "O my son Absalom, my son, my son Absalom! (2 Samuel 18:33, *NRSV*)."

It matters not the child's crime. The name of the child and the relationship will well up out of the parent's loving heart.

So think of it this way, we are God's Absaloms. Though we are dead in trespasses and sins, our God, our Abba Father, our Mother God, is rich in mercy, bends over us, and loves us with a parent's great love.

That is grace—the active, compassionate, redeeming love of God. But that grace must be received *through faith*.

Faith is openness toward God. It is the decision to accept what God gives, to allow God to work *in* one as he has worked *for* one. It is opening one's whole being to the incoming of God as the Saviour of life; it is the total response of the human spirit to the command of God as the Lord of Life. It is in the fullest sense an attitude of trust in God (MacKay, p. 105).

Salvation faith is our acceptance of the fact that the death of Jesus Christ is for us. By his rich mercy and great love, God has given us his son as a sufficient sacrifice, and through the death of his son has taken away our guilt. If we will accept this fact through faith, then we will rise from the death of our guilt, condemnation, selfishness, and sin into a new life of liberty and sonship—into a life that will never see eternal death.

And, amazingly, there is even more than that. If we will put our trust in Christ, not only will he save us and deliver us from our sins and from eternal death, he will come into our dead lives, do away with our deadness, and quicken us to life, joy, hope, and meaning now.

This is what Paul was saying to the Romans: "There is therefore now no condemnation for those who are in Christ Jesus. For the law of the Spirit of life in Christ Jesus has set me free from the law of sin and death" (Romans 8:1-2). Christ will move into every crook and cranny of our inner life to deliver us from bondage and corruption, from habits and destructive appetites of the mind. He will make us new creatures.

That witness comes from all sorts of directions. Here it is from a person named Linda who has given me permission to share her story and a letter she wrote.

Because of the love and care of young couples in our church, Linda has received the rich mercy of God in Jesus Christ. She has been literally saved, not only spiritually, from being "dead in trespasses and sin" as Paul would put it, but saved from being a homeless person, a person without a job, and a life of despair, with no hope for her and her three children.

She publicly professed her faith in a worship service in our church, and I baptized her and her three daughters. I wish you could know her personally and share her joy. This is an expression of it in a note that she wrote to us.

I am not good with words but I know good words when I see them: Jesus Christ and Christ United Methodist Church. Since I have given myself and the girls to the Lord, my life is continuing to change—for the better. I was so blind, but now I can see and follow the light. With the Lord working through so many people in the church and the committee of Project Home Again, I now have a car and a job. Food was given, clothes, the time of others, prayers, diapers, and many other things we were in need of. I am so thankful to all of you. Many prayers have been answered and all I had to do was ask. How simple and great! I've put my life and my children in the hands of the Lord, and now I am "A perfect example—That There Is A God." Please continue to keep my family in your prayers. I walk in the way of the Lord and it's a beautiful day to be alive and a member of this church. I will never be able to thank you all enough. All I can do is show my thanks—and I will. God bless you all—

The Malone Girls.

Well that says it, and that proves it. "For by grace you have been saved through faith; and this is not your own doing, it is the gift of God—not because of works, lest any man should boast."

Reflecting and Recording

Paul described God in this fashion: "God, who is rich in mercy, out of the great love with which he loved us . . . ." (Ephesians 2:4). Spend a few minutes thinking about God with this two-phrase description in your mind: "rich in mercy . . . great in love."

***

Now think of the cross as the ultimate expression of God who is "rich in mercy" and "great in love." In your mind, stand for a couple of minutes before the cross with Jesus dying on it.

***

Write a brief prayer, telling God what you feel about the cross, and thank God for what the cross means to you.

During the Day

Continue to pray the flash prayer: "Thank you, Christ, for your forgiveness, and for making me alive."

If you are sharing this workbook with a study group, you should be meeting today or tonight. Make plans to attend. At some mealtime today, when you are offering thanks for your food, pray for the people who are sharing this study with you, and with whom you will be meeting.

WEEK ONE
Group Meeting

Note to the group leader: Locate a Polaroid camera to take to this meeting. Maybe someone in the group has one if you do not.

Introduction

These group sessions will be most meaningful as they reflect the experience of all the participants. This guide is simply an effort to facilitate personal sharing. Therefore, I encourage you to not be too rigid in following the suggestions below.

The leader, especially, should seek to be sensitive to what is going on in the lives of the participants and to help focus the group's sharing on those experiences.

One other thing that I want to call to the attention of the leaders. Ideas are important. We should wrestle with new ideas as well as with ideas with which we disagree. It is important, however, that the group meeting not become a debate about ideas. The emphasis should be on the persons in the group and their experiences, feelings, and meanings.

The very fact that you are addressing the subject of the Christian Walk means that we are at difference places on the journey. That should be acknowledged, affirmed, and celebrated. The sooner and more freely each person shares personally, the more helpful you will all be to each other. As the group comes to the place where all members can share honestly and openly what is happening in their lives, the experience will become increasingly meaningful.

Sharing Together

1. You may begin your sharing together by allowing time for each person in the group to share his or her most meaningful day with the workbook this week. The leader should be the first to share. Tell why that particular day was so meaningful.

2. Now share your most difficult day, telling what you experienced and why it was so difficult.

3. Spend some time talking about persons' responses to the question, "If I get to where I am going, will I be where I want to be?"

4. Invite two or three persons to share their story of Christ's initial call to them.

5. Invite two or three persons to share the call of Christ during the past few months.

6. Discuss the idea of being "dead in trespasses and sin." How have you experienced it in your life and/or seen it in the lives of others?

7. Discuss the idea of "being made alive in Christ." How have you experienced it in your life and/or in the life of others?

Praying Together

Each week the group is asked to pray together. Corporate prayer is one of the great blessings of Christian community. There is power in corporate prayer, and it is important that this dimension be included in our shared pilgrimage.

It is also important that you feel comfortable in this and that no pressure be placed on anyone to pray aloud. *Silent* corporate prayer may be as vital and meaningful as verbal corporate prayer. God does not need to hear our verbal words to hear our prayers. Silence, where thinking is centered and attention is focused, may provide our deepest periods of prayer.

There is power, however, whenever members of a community on a common journey verbalize their thoughts and feelings to God in the presence of their fellow pilgrims.

I would suggest strongly that verbal prayers should be offered spontaneously as a person chooses to pray aloud—not "let's go around the circle now, and each one pray."

Other suggestions for this time of praying together will be given each week. The leader for the week should regard these only as suggestions. What is happening in the meeting—the mood, the needs that are expressed, the timing—should determine the direction of the group praying together. Here are some possibilities for this closing period.

1. Invite group members to spend time in silent prayer. Invite them to think about each person in the group and offer a one-sentence silent prayer for each person, basing their prayers on what that person may have shared in the meeting, or what they know otherwise about that person. (The leader should judge the time by his or her own practice of this exercise.)

2. Let the leader close with a verbal prayer or contact someone ahead of time to offer a closing prayer.

Picture Taking

Before everyone leaves, take a picture of each person in the group. Then turn the pictures face down on the table and let each person take one home. This is the person for whom each group member will pray specifically this week.

Before you go, take a few minutes to visit with the person whose picture you chose, getting to know him or her better. Ask if there are things coming up in that person's life about which you might pray.

Bring the pictures back to the group meeting each week, shuffle them face down, and let each person select a new person for whom to pray during the following week.

Walk In Christ

DAY ONE
"Why, That Must Be Jesus"

From now on, therefore, we regard no one from a human point of view; even though we once knew Christ from a human point of view, we know him no longer in that way. So if anyone is in Christ, there is a new creation: everything old has passed away; see, everything has become new! All this is from God, who reconciled us to himself through Christ, and has given us the ministry of reconciliation; that is, in Christ God was reconciling the world to himself, not counting their trespasses against them, and entrusting the message of reconciliation to us. So we are ambassadors for Christ, since God is making his appeal through us; we entreat you on behalf of Christ, be reconciled to God. For our sake he made him to be sin who knew no sin, so that in him we might become the righteousness of God.   2 Corinthians 5:16-21, *NRSV*

THREE-YEAR-OLD RYAN AND HIS FIVE-YEAR-OLD SISTER LISA were playing on the floor following a family dinner. The adults were trying to have conversation. Lisa opened her new toy nurse's kit and convinced Ryan to be her patient. She took the little stethoscope and placed it on her brother's heart and listened intently as good nurses do. Suddenly she announced, "I hear somebody walking around in there."

The adults smiled at this, but Ryan, answered matter-of-factly, "Why, that must be Jesus."

That is the amazing promise, and one of the central claims of the Christian Gospel: that Christ may live in us. Indeed that is Paul's definition of a Christian—a person in Christ.

Paul wrote to the Corinthians, "If anyone is in Christ, he is a new creation; the old has passed away, behold, the new has come" (2 Corinthians 5:17).

To the Colossians Paul said, "As therefore you received Christ Jesus the Lord, so live in him . . . " (Colossians 2:6). The King James has it, "As ye have therefore received Christ Jesus the Lord, so walk ye in him . . . ."

To lay a firm foundation for our Christian Walk, we need to explore our spiritual relationship with Christ, which Paul characterized as being in Christ.

Students of Pauline thought, as different from one another as Adolph Deissmann and Albert Schweitzer, are agreed that the phrase *in Christ* is the central category of Paul's thinking. The phrase is used by Paul in his letters at least 169 times.

What does Paul mean by this vital image? I've written a book on the subject entitled Alive in Christ. Hundreds of other books have been written on the theme. It is, therefore, a bit presumptuous to seek to lay a foundation in such scant space, but we must try. What does it mean to be in Christ?

It means first, a new status. To be in Christ is to become a new creation, as Paul puts it in our text. Look at the way Phillips translates the words from 2 Corinthians: "For if a man is in Christ he becomes a new person altogether—the past is finished and gone, everything has become fresh and new." And The New English Bible translates it: "When anyone is united to Christ, there is a new world; the old order has gone, and a new order has already begun."

This new status is the definitive aspect of our existence. I like the way Elva McAllaster put it in her introduction to *Free to Be Single*.

I am a believer.

That is the one most significant fact about me. Not that I'm poet, teacher, counselor, woman. Not that I love outdoor nature, love to hike, enjoy travel. Not that I know certain wonderful human beings. Not anything else. The rest is peripheral, subsidiary, radiating out from the hub like spokes from a wheel.

"I believe in God the Father Almighty, Maker of heaven and earth, and in Jesus Christ his only Son our Lord . . . .

Everything else I have to say on any topic has to acknowledge this primacy.

So it is. To be a believer is the identifying fact of one's being a Christian. But I would add to that: The primary aspect of our total existence as Christians is to be *in Christ*.

Reflecting and Recording

Spend some time reflecting on this question: "Is there a difference between being a believer and being *in Christ?*"

***

During the Day

Copy this verse on a piece of paper that you can carry with you every day this week. "If anyone is in Christ, he is a new creation; the old has passed away, behold the new has come." At those times when you have been praying flash prayers this past week, read this verse of scripture. By the end of the week, you will have memorized it.

DAY TWO
The Definitive Word

A HOTEL CLERK RECEIVED A LONG-DISTANCE PHONE CALL about an overnight reservation. "Do you want a room with a tub or a shower?" the clerk asked.

"What's the difference?" the caller replied.

"Well," came the officious response, "with a tub, you sit down."

Being in Christ is more than just another way of talking about the Christian experience; it is the definitive word. To be in Christ is to have our status in the very life of God. It is to live a God-centered existence.

Look at Phillips' translation of Paul's word to the Corinthians:

> The very spring of our actions is the love of Christ. We look at it like this: if one died for all men then, in a sense, they all died, and his purpose in dying for them is that their lives should now be no longer lived for themselves but for him who died and was raised to life for them. This means that our knowledge of men can no longer be based on their outward lives (indeed, even though we knew Christ as a man we do not know him like that any longer). For if a man is in Christ he becomes a new person altogether—the past is finished and gone, everything has become fresh and new. —2 Corinthians 5:14-17, *PHILLIPS*

Note what may be appear to be a superficial fact. To be in Christ means more than being a believer and far more than being in the Church. Being in the Church is important, but we can be in the Church, in the ways we normally perceive that, without being in Christ. In fact, there are thousands, perhaps millions, of people who are members of the Church, who see themselves as *in* the Church, but do not have the faintest notion about what it means to be in Christ. The truth is they are not really in the Church—they are members, but they are not in the Church.

The Church is the body of Christ. But Christ is greater than the Church. It is through a relationship to Christ that a person becomes related to the Church that is his body. The Church is the reality, the setting, the fellowship where Christ's fullness appears. But the Church does not exhaust Christ and it does not bind or limit Christ. A person is really related to the Church because he is in Christ.

So being "in Christ" means more than being a member of the Church.

To be in Christ means an individual spiritual renewal. It means that we become a new creation, or a new person, as Paul put it.

The scripture is full of this kind of reference. So it is quite meaningless to speak of anyone being in Christ who has not been made alive, as Paul says in 1 Corinthians (chapter 15). Paul also talks about those who were destined to be God's children through Jesus Christ (Ephesians 1:5), and about those persons who were made alive together with Christ (1 Corinthians 15:22) and are raised up with him and made to sit with him in the heavenly places in Christ Jesus (Ephesians 2:6). Such persons organize and determine all their attitudes and actions from their new center which is Jesus Christ.

I now have a more graphic picture of that than I ever had before. In early 1990, my wife Jerry gave her brother Randy a bone marrow transplant. The malignancy was so dominant in his lymphatic system, the doctors said a transplant was the only hope.

All sorts of amazing and beautiful things happened. The doctors were brutally honest. It was going to be tough for Randy; he was going to be brought to the door of death as all his marrow was destroyed and his immune system reduced to zero before he received the transplant. Even after that, if the transplant worked, he would still be flirting with death for a long time because he would be vulnerable to all germs since he would have no immunity to them. Yet, his only hope was the transplant.

What rejoicing there was when it was discovered that Jerry was a perfect match for the transplant. Though it was a painful procedure for Jerry, that took far longer than we anticipated, few folks can know the joy she has known—to literally give life to someone who was dying.

I think I will never forget, and I am sure Jerry and Randy will never forget, February 1, 1990, the day when the doctors made the transplant. Jerry was in a hospital room down the hall from Randy. As she was coming out from the anesthesia, her marrow was being fed into Randy's system. I was back and forth between the rooms during that entire six-hour procedure.

When the last drop of the liter of marrow had gone into his system, the nurse took the IV bag down and said, "That's it, Randy, this is your new birthday. You've been given a new life."

Wow! I can only imagine the joy of Randy and Jerry and the special oneness they now have: her life creating life in him. And it is marvelous to hear them talk about her "marrow" in him. He jokingly blames her for his bad moods, anger, or emotional outbursts. The truth is, he would not be alive without her marrow creating a whole new immune system in him.

That is suggestive of the opportunity that is ours with Christ. Receiving him, and cultivating his presence, we have a new status. We now have a Christ-centered existence. Christ dwells in us, permeating the marrow of our being. It is his life that creates new life in us. We are who we are as Christians because of the personal love of God that comes to us in Jesus Christ.

Reflecting and Recording

Spend some time trying to come up with some images, out of human experience, such as Jerry's bone marrow gift to Randy, that may help to illumine this mysterious, but powerfully real, fact that Christ lives in us, that we are alive in him.

During the Day

Continue your flash prayer repetition of the verse from 2 Corinthians that you wrote down on a slip of paper yesterday.

DAY THREE
A New Style

THE PAST TWO DAYS WE HAVE BEEN CONSIDERING THE FACT that being *in Christ* gives us a new status. Also, persons in Christ have a new style. We become persons in whom a new principle of life has been implanted.

Return to the image of the bone marrow transplant. The doctors insisted that Jerry be at the hospital a week before the transplant was to take place. They would not begin the massive chemical destruction of Randy's diseased marrow until they knew Jerry was physically well and on the site. They wanted to be certain that when Randy's blood count was down to almost nothing, they could inject the new life-producing marrow from Jerry. Her marrow was the new life principle that would give Randy life.

The indwelling presence of Christ is the Christian's life principle, giving us a distinctive style. We may look at that in two ways: *imitation* and *immersion*.

There is a sense in which the Christian Walk is an imitation of Christ, a call to walk as Christ walked. That is the basic content of this workbook—imitating Christ, walking as Christ walked.

We do act our way into Christlikeness. Paul admonished the Colossians:

As ye have therefore received Christ Jesus the Lord, *so* walk ye in him: rooted and built up in him, and established in the faith, as ye have been taught, abounding therein with thanksgiving.   —Colossians 2:6-7, *KJV*

Phillips provides this translation:

Just as you received Christ, so go on living in him—in simple faith. Grow out of him as a plant grows out of the soil it is planted in, becoming more and more sure of the faith as you were taught it, and your lives will overflow with joy and thankfulness.   —Colossians 2:6-7, *PHILLIPS*

It is a challenging image. We grow out of Christ as a plant grows out of the soil in which it is planted. We act our way into Christlikeness.

In his sermon "You're Better Than You Think," Mark Trotter tells about a man named Harry Kahn who has acted like Abraham Lincoln so long that he is even beginning to look like Lincoln. He lives in Mt. Pulaski, Illinois, not far from Springfield, where Lincoln lived. Several years ago, they had a centennial in Mt. Pulaski, and all the men were asked to grow beards. Harry Hahn, who is six feet and four inches tall and weighs 180 pounds, discovered that when he grew his beard he looked a lot like Abraham Lincoln. He was the same size, had the same lines in his face, and pretty soon, people were saying, "Hey, here comes Abe Lincoln!"

That inspired Harry Hahn to buy a long coat and a top hat and some nineteenth-century looking boots and to start making appearances as "Abe Lincoln" at fairs, school assemblies, and service clubs.

Harry Hahn became so fascinated with Abe Lincoln that he began to collect all the books that he could find about Mr. Lincoln. He read, and continues to read, all about Lincoln. He memorized Lincoln's speeches and anecdotes.

When he is out in public, Harry Hahn is especially conscious of who he is supposed to be. He has "put on" Abraham Lincoln. He wants to be more and more like Lincoln. He says he tries to be dignified and kind and human. He tries to be humble. People in Springfield say, "He's even beginning to walk like Abraham Lincoln."

Mark Trotter's story reminds us that there are all sorts of legends and fairy tales about people who pretended to be someone they really were not, until one day they actually became that person they pretended to be. And there is truth in that. Someone may say that it's hypocrisy, pretending to be someone you really aren't. But not in the Christian Walk—when we walk in Christ, we seek to walk as Christ would walk. And, as Martin Luther would say, "We actually become little Christs."

That is what we will seek to do through this workbook: to act our way, by imitation of Christ, into Christlikeness.

Reflecting and Recording

Think of a person you consider to be "Christlike." Name and describe that person here:

Think about that person now, asking the question, "How did he or she become Christlike—by walking as Christ walked?"

***

During the Day

Continue to quote 2 Corinthians 5:17 at flash points during the day. Also, put forth intentional effort today, in all circumstances and relationships, to act Christlike.

DAY FOUR
"Little Christs"

MARTIN LUTHER REFERRED TO CHRISTIANS AS "LITTLE CHRISTS." That is the reason we must go beyond imitation of Christ to *immersion* in Christ. That is where I begin this discussion about style: *Persons in Christ have a new principle implanted within them.*

I have heard it said somewhere that "Conversion to Christ without immersion in Christ is a perversion of the Gospel." To that I would add two clear, direct sentences from John MacKay, a former Dean of Princeton Theological Seminary: "We receive Jesus Christ without cost because of what He has done for us, but it becomes costly business to receive him, because of what He will do in us." And then the second sentence, "God's free grace in Jesus Christ, to which faith responds, becomes costly grace when Christ takes command" (MacKay, p. 111).

What that means in a practical way is that our choice is not whether we will become new persons or not; that is a matter of grace. Christ makes us new creatures. Our choice is whether we will *choose* to start to become new persons. Do you see the difference? We do not choose to become new persons; that's a work of grace within our life. We choose to start to become new persons. And the start requires two things. It requires *imitation* and *immersion*. We begin to walk as we think Christ would have us walk, and we immerse ourselves in Christ—that is, we surrender ourselves to his spirit within, and allow his grace to make us in fact the new persons we already are in principle.

Here is a powerful witness—letters from Von Davis, a death-row inmate. They were written to George and Ann Gaines, directors of Life Row Ministries, who shared them with me.

From his first letter, we learn something of who Von Davis is.

For the record, I arrived here on death row in absolute confusion, insanely bitter over the obvious injustice, full of hate, lonely and abandoned by friends and most family. If there was a "bottom of the barrel," I was under that. Needless to say, I vehemently questioned the existence of God and all human fairness and morals. Execution would have been a relief.

To avoid a long story, allow me to sum the truth up. Today, twenty months after arriving here, I stand guilty of one fact; that is accepting Jesus Christ as my personal Lord and Saviour!"

That is his background, now the second letter:

Greetings again in Jesus' precious name. My phrase for today "What a Friend we have in Jesus!"

Who else will lift us up when we are below down? Who else will forgive us when we know we've been wrong all our lives? Who else will love us when we didn't love ourselves? Who else has a mansion for all of us to live in? Only our Lord Jesus!

I will tell you right out. He is stirring in my soul like a rumbling volcano, and my love is ready to spill. I am ready to burn up the ears of the lost and discouraged. Ready to manifest the Jesus in me, and let it be known that Jesus is alive!"

Rather clear, isn't it? And simple, though not easy. If a death row inmate can immerse himself in Christ and walk that way, then certainly we can claim the possibility.

Reflecting and Recording

Spend a few minutes reflecting on the personal implication of this truth stated by John MacKay:

We receive Jesus Christ without cost because of what He has done for us, but it becomes costly business to receive him, because of what He will do in us (MacKay, p. 111).

***

Write a few sentences about the possible "costs" because of what Christ may do in you.

During the Day

Continue to quote 2 Corinthians 5:17 at today's flash points. Also, put forth intentional effort today, in all circumstances and relationships, to act Christlike.

DAY FIVE
Stand Fast . . . in Freedom

For freedom Christ has set us free; stand fast therefore, and do not submit
again to a yoke of slavery .   —Galatians 5:1

THE IMAGE OF THE CHRISTIAN WALK is an image of movement, of dynamic
journeying. But here Paul uses a word that suggests not movement, but staunch
immovability. Stand fast, or stand firm is the way most translations have it. J. B.
Phillips makes the stance more solid: "Plant your feet firmly therefore within the
freedom that Christ has won for us, and do not let yourselves be caught again in
the shackles of slavery."

Does it make sense to mix the metaphor? The Christian Walk is a stance of
freedom.

But this stance is not static. Yes, Paul is saying, "Don't be moved out of
your freedom. Stand firm, do not let it be taken away, plant your feet firmly."
But that doesn't mean non-movement; there is nothing status-quo about it.
Nothing is more dynamic than freedom.

Look at a word picture entitled "A Visit From the Buddha: Why Did I Visit
the Magic Monastery?" from *Tales of a Magic Monastery* by Theopane the
Monk.

Well, I am a monk myself, and the strangest thing happened in my monastery.

We had a visit from the Buddha. We prepared for it, and gave him a very
warm, though solemn, welcome. He stayed overnight, but he slipped away
early in the morning. When the monks woke up, they found graffiti all over the
walls. Imagine! And do you know what he wrote? One word—TRIVIA—
TRIVIA—TRIVIA—all over the place.

Well, we were in a rage. But then when I quieted down I looked about and
realized, "Yes, it is true." So much of what I saw was trivia, and most of what I
heard. What is worse, when I closed my eyes, all inside was trivia. For several
weeks this was my experience, and my very efforts to rectify it just made it
worse. I left my monastery and headed for the Magic Monastery.

The Brother showed me around. First, the Hall of Laughter. Everything fed
the flame of laughter, big things and small, sacred, solemn, inconsequential.
Only laughter there.

Next, the Room of Sorrow. The very essence of bitter tears—those of the
bereaved mother, the lonely, depressed. *Only* sorrow here.

Now the Hall of Words. Words upon words, spoken and written. Alone they must have had some sense, but all together—total confusion. I cried out, "Stop! Stop!" but I was only adding words to words.

Next, the great Hall of Silence. Here there is no time.

He took me finally to the Hall of Treasures. "Take anything you want," he whispered.

I chose the heart of Jesus, and with it I am heading back to my monastery.

We have said that to walk in Christ means a new status and a new style. It also means a new source of power rooted in the freedom Christ provides.

The Monk had left his own monastery because there all he saw and heard was trivia. But in the Magic Monastery, nothing satisfied. Then he chose the heart of Jesus and was free to go back to his old monastery. It is an image that fits well into what Paul is saying to the Galatians: "For freedom, Christ has set us free."

Here is the Christian's declaration of freedom. We must stand in the freedom Christ has won for us in order to walk in freedom.

It is first a freedom from our past. It is a freedom of release, and there is power in that.

Some of you may remember a telling quote from a late rock star who died a victim of the drug culture. He said, "People look at my life and think that I am free. I am not free. I just can't stop running."

The first verse of chapter five of Galatians is not an introduction of something new; rather it is the conclusion of what Paul has been talking about in the first four chapters of this letter.

Throughout this Epistle to the Galatians, Paul has been making his case: Salvation is the grace gift of God. We are not worthy of it. We cannot earn it. We are justified—that is, made right—by God's grace and our faith response to that grace. In the cross, Jesus has purchased our pardon, doing for us what we could never do for ourselves.

We will never understand the full impact of this meaning of Christian freedom unless we understand the encompassing nature of sin and evil. Paul knew that sin had not just affected human nature, reducing us to slaves of our passions, and bringing death as we discussed on **DAY SIX** of **WEEK ONE**. Paul knew that sin had affected the entire universe. "We know that the whole creation has been groaning in travail," he said to the Romans (8:22). God had to do something of a cosmic significance. What he did—the gift of himself in his son on the cross—revealed the suffering heart of God. From Adam on, sin has inflicted pain in the heart of God. Humans, and all creation, are in bondage to sin until God's gift of grace, his crucified son, is received in faith to release us.

So our freedom is from our past. And we need that freedom.

Many of us know bondage to some aspect of our history. Something happened in our past, and we've never gotten over it. Maybe it was a divorce. Our marriage went to pieces and ended up in divorce court. We think we might have changed things had we been different, or had we done differently, but it's over now, and the guilt still persists.

Maybe it was an abortion. Years ago, when you were younger, you conceived. You were not married, and the fellow wouldn't follow through on his commitment. You became desperate and you didn't know what to do. So you did what you thought at that time was the best thing to do. And now you wish it hadn't happened; you wish that you had tried to solve the problem differently. But that chance is not yours anymore.

Perhaps it was a relationship to a parent. You became estranged. You are not quite sure about everything that went into that estrangement, but you know that you were trying to be free and your parent was trying to control. You couldn't take the domination any longer, and so you cut the relationship. The way it happened was not good. It was ugly—things were said that should never have been said, and you have never been able to get over that. Nor were your parents able to get over it. But now they are dead, and the reconciliation never came. You bear the pain of that, even though your parents have been dead for years.

The list is almost endless. You know what it is in your life, if it's there, and it is there in many of us. We are in bondage to some aspect of our history. How we need the freedom offered by Christ!

When Helmut Gollwitzer was a professor of the Free University in Berlin, he shared a genteel custom that comes out of his Bavarian homeland. When a guest comes to a place, he or she waits as the host enters and takes his place, waiting until the invitation has been given. And then to this invitation, the guest responds, *"Ich bin so frei—*I take the liberty."

Jesus is the great invitation of God to sinners, to those who stand outside, to those who do not belong: "You may come!" But he also provides the power for you to say, "I take the liberty. Nothing in my past will hold me in its bondage any longer. I take the liberty." Freedom is grace, and to believe is to make use of the freedom presented us through grace. This is a new source of power for those who walk in Christ: freedom from our past.

Reflecting and Recording

Is there some experience in your past that is holding you in bondage from which you are not quite free? If so, make some notes describing and clarifying the bondage. It is important to name the experience, to actually put words on paper. In a mysterious way that we do not understand, the very naming of something that is controlling us gives us power over it. So name your bondage to the past.

Your naming and describing your bondage is an act of confession. Now, in an act of faith and dependency on God's grace, believe and accept Christ's forgiveness and freedom. Verbalize your acceptance in prayer.

During the Day

By now, you should have memorized the new creation text from 2 Corinthians 5:17. Copy this one down in the first person:

> For freedom Christ has set *me* free. I will not let myself be caught again in the shackles of slavery.

Take this with you and read it at those flash prayer times of the day. Also continue to act intentionally in ways that are Christlike.

DAY SIX
Two Pasts

AS CHRISTIANS WE HAVE TWO PASTS. And many times our minds become the battleground as those two pasts war against each other. There is our own past—our history of sin and failure, of sorrow and grief, of estrangement and loneliness. But there is also another past. That past is Christ and what Christ has done. In our history as Christians, there is Bethlehem and Golgotha and the Garden Tomb. So Paul said, "But when the fullness of time had come, God sent his Son, born of a woman, born under the law, in order to redeem those who were under the law, so that we might receive adoption as children" (Galatians 4:4-5, *NRSV*).

My wife Jerry and I had an unforgettable experience that underscored this truth. We had been in Korea and were on our way back, with a stopover in Tokyo. When we were in the International Boarding Lounge in Seoul, with a crowd of people waiting to board, we saw three young servicemen in charge of six little babies. We engaged them in conversation and learned that an adoption agency was giving them a free trip home and a free vacation to deliver these little babies to the United States. Each young soldier was responsible for two babies.

Jerry has a real maternal instinct, and before I knew what was happening, we were in charge of one of those babies. As we were flying from Seoul to Tokyo, I was a little afraid that I was about to become a father again. It looked as though Jerry was not going to want to give that baby up.

As I looked at that little Korean baby, there was a kind of sadness that settled over me. She had never known her mother or father; she would never know who they were. She was leaving her homeland, the place of her birth, and would perhaps never visit it again. It was a sad thought. But as I was reflecting on that painful situation, I happened to notice a little band around the baby's arm and I looked at it. On that little bracelet was written Mr. and Mrs. Fred Merchant, and an address in Pittsburgh, Pennsylvania.

Then it happened. My sadness turned to joy. Two people, thousands of miles from Seoul, were adopting this little one in love. While she was leaving her homeland, and would never see her natural parents, she was going into the deliberate love and solid commitment of two people who had chosen to be her parents. She had been deliberately chosen—adopted.

That is a picture of what has been done for us in Jesus Christ.

You see, we have a history. A divine history is a part of our past. We have been adopted by Christ. Christ has taken our sin upon himself, he has died our death, and made our grave his grave. That is the unbelievable divine history out of which we come, which we cannot undo, out of which we can only draw the consequences for our life. Our earlier history, our origin, our point of departure is Christ.

Helmut Gollwitzer, whom I quoted earlier and who inspired this train of thought, used an illuminating image at this point. He says, "As the racer must have solid footing at the start of the race in order to get away fast, so Paul plants our foot on this divine history—for the whole new year, and for every day of the year. This is true: The other past is no longer yours; leave it behind. *This* past in Christ—it can and shall control your future" (Littel, p. 79).

Reflecting and Recording

Looking back over your life, locate some personal experience in which you were chosen. Relish the memory of that experience. Try to get in touch with your feelings and thought when it happened.

***

Looking back at that experience, what difference did it make in your life?

***

We have been chosen by Christ, bought with a price. Write a prayer of gratitude for your being chosen by God.

During the Day

Continue to affirm your freedom by using the verse copied yesterday. Also continue to deliberately seek to act in a Christlike manner.

DAY SEVEN

Freedom to Be Me

OUR FREEDOM IS A NEW SOURCE OF STRENGTH because it is a freedom from the past. We have two pasts. One is our past of sin and bondage; the other is our past of divine intervention in which Christ adopted us and set us free. To claim that divine past is a source of power.

This new source of power that comes from freedom in Christ expresses itself in another way: *freedom to be me.* Paul put it this way:

> With eyes wide open to the mercies of God, I beg you, my brothers, as an act of intelligent worship, to give him your bodies, as a living sacrifice, consecrated to him and acceptable by him. Don't let the world around you squeeze you into its own mold, but let God remold your minds from within, so that you will prove in practice that the plan of God for you is good, meets all his demands and moves toward the goal of true maturity.
>
> —Romans 12:1-2, *PHILLIPS*

To walk in Christ means we are free to be *me*, free to be real. That's not as easy as it sounds. There are powers and persons who would rob us of our freedom to be who we are. There is constant pressure for us to be something we aren't.

It even happens in the bonds of matrimony. A woman was talking about her marriage. "We've been married for five years," she said, "and we've never had a quarrel. If a difference of opinion arises, and I am right, my husband gives in."

"But what if he's right?" came the question.

The response, "Oh, that hasn't happened yet!"

The nature of the liberty in which we are to stand as Christians is a freedom to be me—a freedom to be you.

In two encounters Jesus had during Holy Week, the question of his identity was raised. The chief priests and the scribes brought Jesus before their council, and they said to him, "If you are the Christ, tell us." What an onslaught to Jesus' identity. But Jesus was not threatened. "If I tell you, he said, "you will not believe." (See Luke 22.)

Do you get the picture? Jesus is not going to be drawn into that kind of controversy. He knows who he is, and he knows it so well that he's not even willing to argue with the chief priests and the scribes. The same sort of thing happened before Pilate. Pilate asked him, "Are you the King of the Jews?"

Can't you imagine how Pilate was disarmed? How the whole assembly was disarmed? Without stuttering, without hesitation, Jesus said simply, "You have said so." And I have an idea that he said it without the slightest expression of emotion or anger or argumentativeness. Jesus knew who he was, was free to be who he was, and did not allow others to threaten or manipulate his identity.

Here is the truth in one cryptic sentence. "You will make a lousy anybody else, but you are the best you in existence."

Twila Paris has written a wonderful song entitled "The Warrior Is a Child."

> Lately I've been winnin' battles left and right.
> But even winners can get wounded in the fight.
> People say that I am amazin',
> strong beyond my years;
> They don't see inside of me
> I'm hidin' all the tears.

> They don't know that I go runnin' home when I fall down.
> They don't know who picks me up when no one is around.
> I drop my sword and cry for just awhile
> 'cause deep inside this armor,
> the warrior is a child.

Of course the warrior is a child, and we know that. We know that we are all a unique mixture of the warrior and the child. How that's put together, and all the other aspects of our being, makes us the unique, unrepeatable miracles of God that we are. And Christ gives us the freedom to be those unique selves.

Reflecting and Recording

List three situations in which you find it difficult to be yourself, to be real.

_____

_____

_____

Are there persons with whom it is difficult to be yourself? Name them.

_____

_____

_____

Reflect on whether it is the situations or persons in them or yourself that need to change in order for you to have the freedom to be yourself in those situations.

***

Reflect on the decisions that you may have to make, or what specific actions you may have to take in order to be yourself in the situations and with the persons named.

***

Name the one action you are going to take, starting now, to exercise your freedom to be yourself.

***

During the Day

Continue to affirm your freedom by repeating the verse from Galatians 5. In every situation and relationship, exercise your freedom to be yourself.

If you are in a study group using this workbook, prepare for your meeting and pray for those sharing with you.

WEEK TWO

Group Meeting

Introduction

Participation in a group such as this is a covenant relationship. You will profit the most as you keep the daily discipline of the thirty-minute period and as you faithfully attend these weekly meetings. Do not feel guilty if you have to miss a day in the workbook, or be discouraged if you are not able to give the full thirty minutes in daily discipline. Don't hesitate sharing that with the group. We may learn something about ourselves as we share. We may discover, for instance, that we are unconsciously afraid of dealing with the content of a particular day because of what is required and what it reveals about us. Be patient with yourself and always be open to what God may be seeking to teach you.

Our growth, in part, hinges upon our group participation, so share as openly and honestly as you can. Listen to what persons are saying. Sometimes there is meaning beyond the surface of their words that you may pick up if you are really attentive.

Being a sensitive participant in this fashion is crucial. Responding immediately to the feelings we pick up is also crucial. Sometimes it is important for the group to focus its entire attention upon a particular individual. If some need or concern is expressed, it may be appropriate for the leader to ask the group to enter into a brief period of special prayer for the persons or concerns revealed. Participants should not always depend upon the leader for this kind of sensitivity, for the leader may miss it. Even if you aren't the leader, do not hesitate to ask the group to join you in special prayer. This praying may be silent, or some person may wish to lead the group in prayer.

Remember, you have a contribution to make to the group. What you consider trivial or unimportant may be just what another person needs to hear. We are not seeking to be profound, but simply to share our experience.

Sharing Together

Note: It may not be possible in this time frame to use all these suggestions. The leader should select what will be most beneficial to the group. It is important that the leader be thoroughly familiar with these suggestions in order to move through them selectively according to the direction in which the group is moving and according to the time available. The leader should plan ahead, but do not hesitate to change your plan according to the nature of the sharing that takes place and the needs that emerge.

1. Open your time together with the leader offering a brief prayer of thanksgiving for the opportunity of sharing with the group and of petition for openness and loving in sharing and responding to each other.
2. Let each person share the most meaningful day in this week's workbook adventure.
3. Now share the most difficult day and tell why it was difficult.
4. Discuss the difference between being a believer and being in Christ.
5. Invite persons to share the images of being alive in Christ that come to them as they reflected on **DAY TWO** of this week.
6. Spend some time talking about what it means to *act our way* into Christlikeness.
7. Invite as many persons who will to share a personal experience of being chosen and how that relates to being chosen by Christ.
8. Spend the balance of the time sharing personally about the meaning of freedom in Christ, both freedom from the past and freedom to be yourself.

Praying Together

As stated last week, the effectiveness of this group and the quality of relationship will be enhanced by a commitment to pray for each other by name each day. If you have the pictures of each other, as requested last week, put these pictures face down on a table and let each person select a picture. This person will be the focus of special prayer for the week. Bring the photos back next week, shuffle them and draw again. Continue this throughout your pilgrimage together. Looking at a person's picture as you pray for that person will add meaning. Having the picture will also remind you that you are to give special prayer attention to this person during the week.

1. Praying corporately each week is a special ministry. Take some time now for a period of verbal prayer, allowing each person to mention any special needs he

or she wishes to share with the entire group. Each person might consider whether he or she should share some experience of the past from which they need to be freed (**DAY FIVE**), or some present personal or family need.

2. Invite two or three persons who are willing to share the prayers they wrote on **DAY SIX** in gratitude for being chosen by God.

3. Close your time by praying together the great prayer of the church, the Lord's Prayer. As you pray this prayer, remember that you are linking yourselves with all Christians of all time in universal intercession.

Words of Encouragement

Here are some of my thoughts as you begin the third week of this journey.

1. Discipline is an important dimension of life. Discipline is not slavish rigidity, but an ordering of life that enables you to control your circumstances rather than being controlled by them. For most people, a designated time of prayer is essential for building a life of prayer.

2. If you have not yet established a regular time for both your prayer time and to use this workbook, try to find the right time for you this week. Experiment with the morning, after work, during lunch hour, or before retiring. Find the time that seems best for you.

3. If you discover that you can't cover all the workbook material and exercises given for a day, do not berate yourself. Get what you can out of what you do. There is no point in rushing over three or four steps or principles if you cannot think deeply. Consider them seriously one by one, and move only as far as you can.

4. Intellectual assent to a great principle or possibility is important, but it does us little good until we act upon it—until we say yes in our minds, and live it out in relationships.

5. Don't hesitate to make decisions and resolves, but do not condemn yourself if you fail. God is patient and wants us to be patient with ourselves.

Walk in Newness of Life

DAY ONE
God Is Faithful

For we know that if the earthly tent we live in is destroyed, we have a building from God, a house not made with hands, eternal in the heavens. For in this tent we groan, longing to be clothed with our heavenly dwelling—if indeed, when we have taken it off we will not be found naked. For while we are still in this tent, we groan under our burden, because we wish not to be unclothed but to be further clothed, so that what is mortal may be swallowed up by life. He who has prepared us for this very thing is God, who has given us the Spirit as a guarantee. So we are always confident; even though we know that while we are at home in the body we are away from the Lord—for we walk by faith, not by sight.

—2 Corinthians 5:1-7, NRSV

THE CHRISTIAN WALK IS A WALK OF FAITH, based on the fact that God is faithful. This is the great affirmation Paul is making to the Corinthians. He makes it in the context of our most anguishing questions: What happens to us when we die? Is there life after death? What is the Christian's hope beyond death?

Paul minces no words in answering those questions. He says it as clearly, as directly, as simply as he can: "For we know that if the earthly tent we live in is destroyed, we have a building from God, a house not made with hands, eternal in the heavens."

Then he elaborates on what he said. He talks about this life of ours—our groaning, our tribulation, our sighings with anxiety. Paul is saying that we are vulnerable, that we are open to every onslaught of disease and moral infection, and open to every sorrow and grief. In fact, he uses the image of nakedness. He says the reason we groan and long to put on our heavenly dwelling is that by putting it on, we may not be found naked. He continues that image, suggesting that while we live in this tent, that is, while we are in this life, we sigh with anxiety because we want to be fully clothed, fully protected, and we aren't.

God is faithful. God is going to take these earthly tents that we live in, and give us a house not made with hands, eternal in the heavens.

We could talk about God's faithfulness in a lot of different ways. Indeed, Paul does. Is there a more bracing word than his word to the Philippians: "And I am sure that he who began a good work in you will bring it to completion at the day of Jesus Christ" (Philippians 1:6). We can count on it.

Oh, I know how weary we can become in well-doing. We labor in our righteous causes, and nothing seems to change, but we need to remember: God doesn't settle all his debts on Friday. God's payday is not on a weekly or a monthly or even an annual cycle. But God's payday is certain. God is faithful, and we can count on it. That is the way that Paul counseled the Galatians: "And let us not grow weary in well-doing, for in due season we shall reap, if we do not lose heart" (Galatians 6:9).

Not long ago, I received a letter from a young woman in my congregation. She had come to me for counseling. Her big concern was her husband. We concluded that her ministry was that of prayer. So, she prayed. Faithfully, she prayed, and God was faithful. Her husband decided to go to a Walk to Emmaus, a weekend renewal experience. That was a miracle within itself, and the beginning of other miracles. Here is a letter she wrote.

Dear Maxie and Jerry:

I know you have experienced many miracle stories from Emmaus, but I wanted to share an update on ours in hopes that it will give you continued strength and power in your dedication to this weekend.

We have a Christ-centered husband and father now. It is everything I've prayed for!

Randy has been waking up each morning since Emmaus, reading his newly purchased Bible and having prayer time. He has started taking his lunch to work so he can come home early to be with us. He has been less stressed out over his job. He has been in close contact with James Loftin (one of our ministers) and we are about to start in a couples growth group. He's very interested in missions. He has been meeting with his reunion group bimonthly. He has been writing notes and letters to people whereas it used to be more "my job." We are sharing Christian thoughts, ideas, and goals.

After my Emmaus, I felt the need to step out and "really tithe" after trusting God like I had never trusted God before. I shared my thoughts with Randy and he was ready also and so *we* increased our pledge together!

The neatest thing is that it's been such a natural, smooth, and *real* change. I'm giving thanks each day that we have this so early in life. Most importantly, I'm looking for all the ways God wants me to respond to others so as to give back the gift we received.

I know that there are countless persons who are on the *not-yet* side, rather than the *victory* side of God's faithfulness. Your spouse is still drinking and you wonder how long you can hang in there. You still do not have a job. It has been months now and the savings are running out, the future looks bleak and so many are dependent upon you. Your son is closing in on thirty and he just left his wife and little daughter, and he won't talk to anyone. Your mother is just hanging on to life in the nursing home, existing but not really living, breathing but not alive, and your financial resources are being drained daily.

I could go on and on. You are on the not-yet side rather than the victory-side of God's faithfulness. It is difficult for you to believe what I am saying. But believe it we must: God is faithful. Not to believe is an awful alternative that offers no hope.

The Christian Walk is a walk of faith based on the fact that God is faithful.

Reflecting and Recording

Record here your present experience of being on the not-yet side of God's faithfulness—an experience of pain, loss, defeat, or trying difficulty in which God's faithfulness has not been proven.

Record here an experience in your own life when God's faithfulness was proven.

If you recorded an experience of God's faithfulness being proven, does that not add strength for you to hold on in faith until God's faithfulness is proven in your present situation?

***

During the Day

Pay special attention today to the world around you—to nature, human achievement and design, relationships—all that happens to you. Seek to discern signs of God's faithfulness.

DAY TWO

By Faith, Not by Sight

NOT ONLY IS GOD FAITHFUL, as we considered yesterday; we are called to be full of faith, too.

Recall the story of Abraham, one of the most moving stories in the Bible. There is no greater demonstration and no clearer picture of faith than the one captured in the words of Abraham to his son Isaac, whom he was preparing to offer as a sacrifice: "God will provide . . . " (Genesis 22:8).

It is hard for us to even imagine that kind of faith. God had commanded Abraham to take his precious son to the land of Moriah and offer him as a sacrifice to God. When they reached Moriah, Abraham stopped, and said to the two men who were with him, "You wait here. We are going to worship and we will come back." So he and Isaac went on. When they arrived at the place of sacrifice, young Isaac asked with natural curiosity, "Daddy, we've got the fire, and we've got the wood. Here is the altar, but where is the lamb for the burnt offering?"

Can you imagine the pain in Abraham's heart? He was thinking, You, my only son, you are the lamb; you are the sacrifice. But instead of saying that, by faith Abraham simply responded, "God will provide."

And you know the rest of the story. Abraham followed through faithfully, prepared the altar, even bound Isaac on it, and got ready with his knife to make that final movement of faith—the sacrifice of his only son. But God called out, stopped his hand, and told him to look around because he had provided an alternative sacrifice.

I like what Abraham did later. In fact, I like how this sort of thing happened over and over again in the Old Testament. When people had an experience with

God, they named that experience and they named the place of the experience. Abraham called the place *Jehovah-jireh,* which means "the Lord will provide."

To walk by faith is to walk in trust, believing that the Lord will provide. And God will. We can count on it, because God is faithful.

I remember these words and thoughts of Barbara Brokhoff.

Some things I've checked [God] on. He said, "Come to me and I will give you rest." And in the words of Horatius Bonar,

"I came to Jesus as I was, weary and worn and sad,

I found in him a resting place, and He has made me glad."

I trusted Him when He said, "I'll give you water of life so you'll never thirst again.—and the writer found, with me,

"I came to Jesus, and I drank Of that life-giving stream;

My thirst was quenched, my soul revived, And now I live in Him."

He said, and I believed Him, "I am the Light of the World."

"I looked to Jesus, and I found In him my Star, my Sun;

And in that light of life I'll walk, Till traveling days are done" (Brokhoff, p. 325.)

Reflecting and Recording

Look back over the past couple of years of your life. Locate an occasion when you were called on to walk by faith, not by sight. Write a few words to remind you of that experience—persons, places, circumstances.

Now spend some time remembering and reliving that experience.

***

What difference has that experience made in your faith walk since?

_____

_____

During the Day

Continue to look for signs of God's faithfulness.

DAY THREE

God Calls Us to Faithfulness

IN THE CHINESE LANGUAGE there are two characters for our word "crisis." Those two characters signify danger and opportunity.

Have you heard the story of the fellow who had been tarred and feathered and was being ridden out of town on a rail? He said, "Gentlemen, if it were not for the honor of the occasion, I'd just as soon walk."

Risk is what makes life exciting. To walk in faith is to risk. But if there is no risk, there is no stimulation. Ultimately, the issue is whether or not we will trust God in the space between the past and the future—and allow God to shape our future. The issue is whether we are going to walk by faith as if there were light, or whether we allow fear, anxiety, dread, and anger to shape our future.

God calls us to faithfulness. Paul said, "It is required in stewards, that a man be found faithful" (1 Corinthians 4:2, *KJV*). He listed faith as a "fruit of the Spirit" in Galatians 5. And John received this revelation from Christ on the island of Patmos:

> Do not fear what you are about to suffer. Behold, the devil is about to throw some of you into prison, that you may be tested, and for ten days you will have tribulation. Be faithful unto death, and I will give you the crown of life.
>
> —Revelation 2:10

I am coming to believe that faithfulness is one of the most important virtues for the Christian. Yet, we do not think of faithfulness with any sort of excitement. It seems to be such a pedestrian virtue. It isn't attractive as love and peace; certainly not as exciting to think about as joy. But it's basic—it's the bedrock upon which our Christian Walk must be built.

It is faithfulness that shines through clearly in one of the strong teachings of Jesus. You remember the story he told about the fellow who was going off for a long time and left his resources to three employees. He gave them one, two, and five talents respectively, and when he came back, he called for an accounting. The one who had received five talents had used his resources well and had doubled his master's holdings. Likewise, the one who had been given two talents had doubled his, but the one who had been given one talent simply hid the money and returned it to his master intact.

The response of the master to the two persons who had done well was this: "Well done, good and faithful servant; you've been faithful over a little, I will set you over much; enter into the joy of your master" (Matthew 25:21).

It interests me that Jesus was not praising success; there are other instances in scripture when he says we can be too intent on success. To be sure, these persons were successful, but that was incidental to what Jesus was teaching. What mattered was their faithfulness, their trustworthiness.

My friend Ellsworth Kalas closed a sermon on one occasion with these words:

When the scores of life are totaled, and God's troops report back home, He will not say, "Well done, you brilliant servant," or "Well done, you ball of fire." No, no; God will say, "Well done, good and faithful servant." In God's lexicon of values, it is faithfulness that makes a star performer (Kalas, August 18, 1985).

Reflecting and Recording

Barbara Brokhoff shares a story, told by Dr. William Holmes Borders, the long-time pastor of the Wheat Street Baptist Church in Atlanta, of two little black boys that are fighting on a street corner.

An elegant white lady came by in a chauffeur-driven limousine, stopped the car, and told them to stop fighting. The boys stopped just long enough to assess where the orders came from, and then when they saw who was giving the command, they decided they didn't have to mind her. Before they went back to slugging it out with each other, one of them said, "Her ain't talkin' to we, 'cause us do not belong to she!" (Brokhoff, p. 323)

To test our faithfulness, we have to keep asking, "Do our actions reflect the One to whom we belong, the one who has given himself in faithfulness to us?"

Spend some time in prayer in response to that question.

During the Day

Be aware of whether or not your actions today reflect the One to whom you belong. Make mental notes (maybe even write them down) of the occasions when there is a clear option to be faithful or unfaithful in your Christian Walk.

DAY FOUR

Walk in Newness of Life

What shall we say then? Are we to continue in sin that grace may abound? By no means! How can we who died to sin still live in it? Do you not know that all of us who have been baptized into Christ Jesus were baptized into his death? We were buried therefore with him by baptism into death, so that as Christ was raised from the dead by the glory of the Father, we too might walk in newness of life.
—Romans 6:1-4

JERRY AND I CELEBRATED OUR THIRTY-THIRD ANNIVERSARY on March 15, 1990. I was in the midst of writing this workbook.

One thing I did in celebration was reread an anniversary gift of years back, a book by Lois Wyse entitled *Love Poems for the Very Married*. If we were very married then, we are very, very married now. In one of her poems, Wyse says:

> You never made
> A lampbase out of a Cracker Jack box,
> An extra room out of an unused closet,
> Or a garden out of a pile of clay.
> All you ever made was
> A woman out of me.

Husbands, wouldn't we all like for our wives to be able to say that to us. "You did what was most important. You fed my hunger for meaning. You accepted my uniqueness. You didn't try to change me. You loved me, and I became who I was meant to be." Wow!

It is not a long way from that to Paul's word to the Romans. In the first five chapters of Romans, Paul has just given his reasoned doctrine of justification by grace through faith. We have absolutely nothing for which to boast, and we can do nothing to receive the favor of God. We talked about this in an earlier section. We can only receive through faith what God has given us. God's righteousness is given us in the death and resurrection of Christ. Everything is grace.

So, Paul begins the sixth chapter of Romans with questions: "What shall we say then? Are we to continue in sin that grace may abound?"

Then he answers adamantly in verse 2: "By no means! How can we who died to sin still live in it?"

Then comes an amazing affirmation and a challenging call. The affirmation is in verse 3: "Do you not know that all of us who have been baptized into Christ Jesus were baptized into his death?" The call is in verse 4: "We were buried therefore with him by baptism into death, so that as Christ was raised from the dead by the glory of the Father, we too might walk in newness of life."

"Walk in newness of life." Because of what Christ has done for us, we are new persons. Now, he says, walk as though you are new persons. Walk in newness of life.

What does it mean to walk in newness of life? To answer that, let's look at another question: How Christian are we Christians?

In 1967, Wilfred Cantwell Smith wrote a book entitled *Questions of Religious Truth*. He concludes with a chapter bearing the title, "Christian—Noun or Adjective." In it, Dr. Smith says that if he is asked if he is *a* Christian, he readily answers, "Yes!" But, if someone asks him if he is *Christian,* using the word as an adjective, "the situation changes radically."

Do you see the point? Do we use Christian as a noun or as an adjective? If someone asked you if you were a Christian, you would say yes. But if they didn't put that little article in there, if they didn't ask if you are a Christian, but rather said "Are you Christian?", you might find that a more searching question, a more disquieting one. "One that undermines my complacency," Dr. Smith said. "Indeed, to ponder it is to be set all a-tremble. The noun is comforting, the adjective demanding."

I know what Dr. Smith is talking about, and so do you. I am a Christian, but I know that I do not always act authentically and consistently Christian. So the noun versus adjective distinction with that word makes me very uncomfortable. I hope it does you. Consider this word from J. A. Davidson.

We are misled when we think of being a Christian and being Christian as matters of achievement. St. Augustine of Hippo, one of the most influential thinkers in Christian history, said that "God deals with us, not as we are, but as we are becoming." Martin Luther reflected this insight many years later when he wrote, "The Christian is not in a state of being, but in one of becoming." Christian-ness, then, is not a condition but a process (Davidson, p. 18).

So, it is a legitimate question: How Christian am I?

Reflecting and Recording

Reflect on the difference between "I am Christian" and "I am a Christian."

***

What is your biggest stumbling block to saying "I am Christian"?

During the Day

Observe your actions and attitudes today. Note those times when what you do, say, or feel, would raise a question about your claim to be a Christian.

DAY FIVE

Add Flavor to Your Kindness

WITH THE QUESTION FROM YESTERDAY—How Christian are we?—as a backdrop, let me suggest some movements for us to make as we walk in newness of life. The first one is to add flavor to your kindness.

I heard a story of a woman from Melbourne, Australia. She was 70 years old when she experienced a dramatic and transforming relationship with Christ. She went to her pastor and told him about her call to serve God. Now what should she do? He didn't know quite what to say, so he told her to go home and pray about it.

Well, she did what he told her to do, and would you believe, she came up with a plan. She bought a batch of 3 x 5 cards and wrote on them, "Are you homesick? Come to my house for tea at four." She listed her address on the bottom of the card. Then she posted these little cards all around the University of Melbourne.

For the next two weeks, this woman had tea ready at four o'clock every afternoon, but nobody came. Then, after a number of weeks, one Indonesian student showed up, homesick and eager to share if only someone would listen and care. He found what he needed.

Soon other students were coming. When this woman died ten years later, there were at least 80 pallbearers at her funeral, from places like India, Pakistan, Indonesia, Malaysia. They had come into a friendship with God through a loving, listening woman who served them tea every day at four o'clock. Clearly, she served more than tea. And it all began because she decided to be kind and when she added flavor to her kindness.

To the Corinthians, Paul writes, "Love is patient and kind . . . " (1 Corinthians 13:4). To the Ephesians he writes, "Be kind to one another, tenderhearted, forgiving one another, as God in Christ forgave you" (Ephesians 4:32). He also listed kindness as one of the fruits of the spirit in Galatians.

Yet, we think too little of kindness as a mark of our Christian Walk. We would hardly think of it as a sign of our newness of life! Quite the opposite, we may consider kindness inane. But when we add flavor to it, when we put it into creative action, it becomes a powerful factor in our discipleship.

Reflecting and Recording

Recall and record your most vivid experience of someone being kind to you.

When was the last time you expressed such kindness to another? If it was some time ago, what does that was say about your Christian Walk?

***

During the Day

Look for opportunities to express kindness today.

———

DAY SIX

Let Goodness Come to Life in You

YESTERDAY WE CONSIDERED KINDNESS as a sign of our walking in newness of life. Today we will consider goodness.

Kindness and goodness are very close together. We often use the words somewhat interchangeably. My friend, Ellsworth Kalas, has shared that a few years ago, he preached about one of his favorite Biblical characters, Barnabas. He called Barnabas "a gardener among human beings" because of the way he nurtured the lives of others and brought out the best in them. In Acts, it is said of him that he was a "good man, full of the Holy Ghost and faith" (chapter 11).

Ellsworth thought, in light of all the kind things Barnabas did, that probably the Greek word to describe him would be that one used for kindness, *chrestotes,* because it seemed that he possessed the sort of goodness that was best measured as kindness.

But when Ellsworth examined the Greek text, he found that his assumption and insight were wrong. The word that described Barnabas was not *chrestotes,* but *agathosune,* which means "strong goodness, virtue equipped at every point."

Barnabas had an aggressive sense of righteousness. When Paul was converted, the Christian community was skeptical of him, and when Paul came to a headquarters meeting, they essentially shut him out. But Barnabas sought him out, brought him to the apostles, and told them what God had done for Paul. Barnabas could easily have settled for being personally sympathetic with Paul, with just visiting him personally, or writing him a supporting letter. Those would have been lovely things to do, but Barnabas exercised strong goodness. He hunted Saul out, pleaded his case with the apostles, and gave him a job to do.

The same thing happened a few years later with John Mark. When Paul and Barnabas had become a missionary team, Mark went along as a sort of intern, a junior assistant. Along the way, the young Mark became homesick, so much so that he left them without a proper farewell. When Paul and Barnabas were ready to start another missionary journey, Barnabas suggested that they give Mark another chance. Paul refused. Barnabas could easily have dropped the matter, gone to Mark, and explained to him kindly that he believed in him, that he had tried to get him another chance, but Paul wouldn't allow it. He could have expressed his regret the whole thing hadn't worked out. Not Barnabas. He possessed the kind of tough goodness that wouldn't give up. He fought for Mark and when Paul refused to give in, Barnabas split with Paul over the issue. Barnabas was a good man, a kind man, but his kindness was reinforced with spiritual muscle. We need just such strong goodness.

Goodness that is a sign of our walk in newness of life is a goodness that is very different from that weak word that we normally see it as. It is a goodness that is transformed into something stronger—not simply being good, but being good for something. The call is to let such goodness come to life in us.

Reflecting and Recording

On **DAYS THREE, FOUR, FIVE,** and **SIX** of **WEEK TWO,** you were to put forth intentional effort to act Christlike. Yesterday, you were asked to express kindness. Have you followed through on these suggestions? Has anything worth noting happened as a result of your effort? Make some notes here.

During the Day

Be deliberate in adding flavor to your kindness and letting goodness take life in you.

DAY SEVEN

Give Compassion a Chance

And Jesus went about all the cities and villages, teaching in their synagogues and preaching the gospel of the kingdom, and healing every disease and every infirmity. When he saw the crowds, he had compassion for them, because they were harassed and helpless, like sheep without a shepherd. Then he said to his disciples, "The harvest is plentiful, but the laborers are few; pray therefore the Lord of the harvest to send out laborers into his harvest."   —Matthew 9:35-38

WE'VE LOOKED AT KINDNESS AND GOODNESS THE PAST TWO DAYS. We look now at compassion. There is a sense in which compassion is kindness and goodness lived with passion.

Compassion was a primary characteristic of Jesus' life. Over and over again in the Gospels, that word is used. One of the most beautiful uses of that word came in reference to Jesus' teaching, preaching and healing. The Gospel writer says, "When he saw the crowds, he had compassion for them, because they were harassed and helpless, like sheep without a shepherd."

He was always reaching out to touch people. He took children in his arms and blessed them. He touched the eyes of a blind man. He touched the body of a leper. He touched the life of Zacchaeus. He touched the life of Simon Peter. He touched the life of Mary Magdalene. He was a person of compassion. He lived goodness and kindness with passion. There were no lines that he did not cross, there was no one for whom he did not die. No one was banished from his love.

Through us today, the living Christ would reach out to men and women, to youth and children, who are in loneliness and despair and sickness and suffering, in weakness and in sin. He would reach out to people in the chains of poverty, in the grip of addiction, and in the prisons of affluence that do not provide the meaning folks are looking for. Still today, the living Christ would reach out in compassion, in goodness and kindness that is lived with passion by us.

Malcolm Muggeridge was a great English writer who became a Christian very late in life. He wrote a book about Mother Teresa of Calcutta entitled *Something Beautiful For God,* and in it he tells about the time in the late 1930's when he was first in Calcutta, a city that was already full of people suffering from a poverty beyond belief.

It was too much; I made off, back to my comfortable flat and a stiff whiskey and soda, to expatiate through the years to come on Bengal's wretched social conditions, and what a scandal it was, and how it was greatly to be hoped that the proper authorities would . . . and so on."

I ran away and stayed away; Mother Teresa moved in and stayed. That was the difference (Muggeridge, p. 22).

That is always the difference that compassion brings, isn't it?

Reflecting and Recording

We've been involved in this study for three weeks. Looking back . . .
What has been the most challenging idea?

The most upsetting thought?

The most comforting or affirming suggestion?

The most puzzling or confusing idea?

The aspect of the Christian Walk you want to work on most?

During the Day

Look for ways to give compassion a chance.

If you are in a study group using this workbook, prepare for your meeting and pray for those sharing with you.

WEEK THREE
Group Meeting

Introduction

Two essential ingredients of Christian fellowship are *feedback* and *follow-up*. Feedback is necessary to keep the group dynamic working positively for all participants. Follow-up is essential to express Christian concern and ministry.

The leader is primarily responsible for feedback in the group. All persons should be encouraged to share their feelings about how the group is functioning.

Listening is crucial. To listen to another, as much as any other action, is a means of affirming that person. When we listen to another, we are saying, "You are important; I value you." It is also crucial to check out meaning, in order that those who are sharing this pilgrimage with us can know that we are really listening to and hearing them. We so often *mis*-hear. "Are you saying _____?" is a good check question. It takes only a couple of persons in a group, who listen and give feedback in this fashion, to set the mood for the group.

Follow-up is the function of everyone. If we listen to what others are saying, we will discover needs and concerns beneath the surface, situations that deserve special prayer and attention. Make notes of these as the group shares. Follow up during the week with a telephone call, a written note of caring and encouragement, a visit. What distinguishes a Christian fellowship is *caring in action*. ("My, how those Christians love one another!") Be sure to follow up each week with others in the group.

Sharing Together

By this time, a significant amount of "knowing" exists in the group. Persons are feeling safe in the group, perhaps more willing to share. Still, there is no place for pressure. The leader, however, should be especially sensitive to those slow to share. Seek gently to coax them out. Every person is a gift to the group and the gift is fully revealed by sharing. Be sure to save at least ten minutes for prayer at the close of this session.

1. Turn to the *Reflecting and Recording* section for **DAY SEVEN** of this past week and spend fifteen to twenty minutes discussing the five questions there. Share personal responses.
2. Invite two or three persons to share experiences in their life when God's faithfulness was proven.

3. Invite two or three persons to share an experience of being called to walk by faith, not by sight, and the difference that experience has made in their faith walk since that time. Then discuss as a group the most common areas where we have to walk by faith.

4. Spend ten to fifteen minutes discussing the word Christian as a noun and as an adjective (from **DAY FOUR** of **WEEK THREE**).

Praying Together

1. The leader should take up the Polaroid pictures of the group, shuffle them, and let each person draw a new one.

2. Invite each member of the group to spend two minutes in quiet prayer for the person whose picture he or she has drawn, focusing on what the person has shared in this meeting.

3. Invite those who wish to share a present experience of being on the not-yet side of God's faithfulness, an experience of pain, loss, defeat, or trying difficulty in which God's faithfulness has not yet been proven.

4. Close the time with sentence prayers, praying specifically about the needs shared by persons.

Saying Yes to Forgiveness

Keepers of the Flame

From now on, therefore, we regard no one from a human point of view; even though we once regarded Christ from a human point of view, we regard him thus no longer. Therefore, if any one is in Christ, he is a new creation; the old has passed away, behold, the new has come. All this is from God, who through Christ reconciled us to himself and gave us the ministry of reconciliation; that is, in Christ God was reconciling the world to himself, not counting their trespasses against them, and entrusting to us the message of reconciliation. So we are ambassadors for Christ, God making his appeal through us. We beseech you on behalf of Christ, be reconciled to God. For our sake he made him to be sin who knew no sin, so that in him we might become the righteousness of God.

—2 Corinthians 5:16-21

I HAVE READ THAT ANTHROPOLOGISTS REPORT that in a certain primitive tribe located deep in the South American jungles the most important role within the tribe is the keeper of the flame. Since fire is so precious and takes such effort to recreate, one member is entrusted with the responsibility of keeping the flame alive.

During the night, the flame keeper adds wood to the fire. He keeps the fire alive whenever the tribe moves to another location, carrying the fire in some vessel in order that the very difficult task of starting a fire under such primitive circumstances might not have to be repeated. His is a vital task.

I've begun to believe that such a role is the most important in every tribe and every culture. I have begun to believe that there must be the keepers of the flame of truth—basic integrity; keepers of the flame of love—care for one another; and keepers of the flame of conviction—willingness to stand for right and justice.

Paul named the one flame that every Christian is to keep alive. "All this is from God, who through Christ reconciled us to himself and gave us the ministry of reconciliation."

Reconciliation—that is the ministry to which we are all called. The dynamic of reconciliation is forgiveness and forgiveness is integral to our Christian Walk.

Most of the persons who come to me for counseling could be healed by forgiveness and reconciliation. I doubt if there is anything more important to emotional mental, spiritual, and physical health than forgiveness. When harbored within, unforgiveness, enmity, and resentment toward others and ourselves will fester and swell, will become poisonous and infect our whole being—our minds, spirits, and bodies.

Harry Emerson Fosdick, one of the most renowned preachers of the twentieth century, suffered a nervous breakdown in his younger days. In his autobiography *The Living of These Days,* he writes: "It was what I did the struggling with that was sick. I, who had thought myself strong, found myself beaten, unable to cope not only with outward circumstances but even with myself."

A big part of his healing came from forgiving and accepting himself.

Reflecting and Recording

Write a one sentence definition of the following words:

Resentment—

Estrangement—

Reconciliation—

Forgiveness—

During the Day

As you move through this day, encountering people you know and love, ask if there is any need for forgiveness and reconciliation in your relationship to each of them.

DAY TWO

Saying Yes to Forgiveness Is Saying Yes to God

CLEMENT OF ALEXANDRIA, ONE OF THE EARLY CHURCH FATHERS, said all Christians should practice being God. When I first read that, it shocked me. Me? *Practice being God?* But the more I thought about it, the more palatable and the more gripping the idea became.

Now don't close your mind, thinking I am being irreverent when I ask, How do I practice being God? If it is an irreverent thought, then I am in good company. Listen to Paul.

> From now on, therefore, we regard no one from a human point of view; even though we once regarded Christ from a human point of view, we regard him thus no longer.   —2 Corinthians 5:16

He was talking about practicing being God—not viewing persons from a human point of view, but from God's point of view. And when we have that perspective, the ministry of reconciliation follows.

Come at it from a slightly different direction. When are we most like God? We are most like God when we are most like Christ. And when are we most like Christ? We find our scriptural answer in this same chapter of Paul's letter.

> For the love of Christ controls us, because we are convinced that one has died for all; therefore all have died. And he died for all, that those who live might live no longer for themselves but for him who for their sake died and was raised.   —2 Corinthians 5:14-15

Instead of saying, "the love of Christ controls us," the King James Version says, "the love of Christ constraineth us." Both words are powerful. The love of Christ controls or constrains. Why? Because we are convinced that Christ died for all.

"We are convinced that (Christ) has died for all." What an encompassing statement! It means that since he has died for all, he has died for each, and that is the great solvent by which the love of God melts our hearts. That is the great proof that Jesus Christ loves me and loves you and loves all of us. If we eliminate or ignore that concept, we have eliminated from our Christian faith the proof, the vindication, of the belief that Christ loves the world.

I have serious reservations about whether we can love Christ in the way that we are called to love him if we do not believe that he loved the world enough to die for it. We may admire him, we may even bow before him, we may see him as the ideal of humanity, and we may even seek to pattern our lives after him. But I doubt if we can, or will, love him as we might and as we should until this affirmation lays hold of us: We are convinced that one (Christ Jesus) has died for all. The love that constraineth, that controls, is the love that died, and that love died for each because it died for all.

I have a friend, Mary Levack, a former Roman Catholic nun who now works as a program director for a Methodist church, whose testimony of this love of Christ for each and for all is powerful. Her father left her mother with 14 children when Mary was only 5 years old. You can imagine what that would do to a little girl—feeling abandoned, unloved, unwanted. She entered the convent when she was young. Two sisters had done so before her.

She told me her story late one night over coffee after I had preached in her church. I was so moved that I asked her to record her testimony on tape and asked her permission to share it.

> I entered the convent for two reasons. One, I felt the Lord calling me to a closer life with him. And two, I was such a scrupulous individual, and needed direction in the depths of my spirit because I did not really understand what this closer walk with the Lord meant for me—I was of the mind that I had to make up for my sins. And so, as a teenager in the middle fifties faced with a time when it came time to do something with my life, I was of the opinion that it would be difficult for me to love one person to the exclusion of all others, and marriage therefore seemed out of the question, even though I felt that was a stronger personal desire than going into the convent. But I needed to make up for my sins, and so I thought God must be calling me into the convent.
>
> Two of my sisters had entered the convent before me. And, having been let into the convent, I was blessed. I found the Lord in a most beautifully intimate way. But I also found community life was very threatening, and five years later I ran away because it was too difficult for me, in the sense that I was in too much inner turmoil. I was very closed-mouthed. I wasn't really a person who shared what was going on inside of her; I didn't know you could do that and be respected for it. So I left the convent.
>
> Because I hadn't been counseled properly I went right into another depression and thought, Well, God, now I've really blown it, I've divorced the

Lord, and I am never going to get to heaven. So I went back into my wounded position and cried and wept and prayed and felt that God moved heaven and earth and Rome, and I was finally accepted back into the convent. And again I was blessed. This time I had a little more help in finding out what was really the source of the problem.

The word of the Lord came to me through a priest to whom I had admitted having entered the convent, among other reasons, for the sake of making up for my sins. When he heard this, he literally wept. And then he said, "Oh, my God, didn't anyone ever tell you Jesus did that. You don't have to do that. You can't do that. Just receive his forgiveness."

Well, at that time I was almost 30 years old and I had just heard the Good News. And, praise God, it was from a Catholic priest.

So when are we most like God? We are most like God when we are most like Christ. And when are we most like Christ? We are most like Christ when we are doing what he did in his extravagant gift of love on Calvary—forgiving.

Reflecting and Recording

Can you put your memory finger on the occasion in your life when you actually received the forgiveness of Christ? If so, describe that experience here. You may want to do it briefly—just making notes. But it is a healing experience to do it as Mary did. So maybe you'll want to make some notes here and take the time now, or later, to write a more complete expression of that experience.

If you can't remember such an experience, spend some time reflecting on these questions: Do I *feel* forgiven? Have I *accepted* with my *heart*, as well as my mind, that Christ forgives me?

***

During the Day

Again, as you move through the day encountering people you know and love, ask if there is any need for forgiveness and reconciliation in your relationship to each of them.

DAY THREE
Say Yes to Forgiveness

IN REFLECTING AND RECORDING YESTERDAY, you were asked to remember the occasion when you actually received the forgiveness of Christ. If it was not possible for you to actually pinpoint an occasion, you were asked to ponder two questions: Do I feel forgiven? Have I accepted with my *heart*, as well as my mind, that I am forgiven?

The exercise raises a serious issue that must be resolved if we are to know freedom and joy in our Christian Walk. While it is not necessary for us to have an explicit forgiveness experience that we can name and date, it is absolutely essential that we know the forgiveness of Christ.

Consider the words from the first twelve verses of Psalm 51.

> Have mercy on me, O God,
> according to they steadfast love;
> according to thy abundant mercy
> blot out my transgressions.
> Wash me thoroughly from my iniquity,
> and cleanse me from my sin!
>
> For I know my transgressions,
> and my sin is ever before me.
> Against thee, thee only, have I sinned,
> and done that which is evil in thy sight,
> so that thou art justified in thy sentence

and blameless in thy judgment.
Behold, I was brought forth in iniquity,
and in sin did my mother conceive me.

Behold, thou desirest truth in the inward being;
therefore teach me wisdom in my secret heart.
Purge me with hyssop, and I shall be clean;
wash me, and I shall be whiter than snow.
Fill me with joy and gladness;
let the bones which thou hast broken rejoice.
Hide thy face from my sins,
and blot out all my iniquities.
Create in me a clean heart, O God,
and put a new and right spirit within me.
Cast me not away from thy presence,
and take not thy holy Spirit from me.
Restore to me the joy of thy salvation,
and uphold me with a willing spirit.

The psalm is credited to David, and is thought to be his prayer after being confronted by Nathan for his sin with Bathsheba and having her husband killed. The cry for forgiveness is an anguishing one. David cannot live without it. Nor can we.

The illuminating word for our discussion is the petition, "Restore to me the joy of thy salvation." The issue is that we cannot know the *joy of salvation* if we do not know our sins are forgiven.

Again, it does not have to be a one-time experience that we can name and date, but it does have to be experienced. I mean we must *know,* in the depths of our souls, that we are accepted and forgiven by Christ if we are to have freedom in our Christian Walk and know the joy of salvation.

We may have a problem at one of two extremes. One, we may think our sins are too great to be forgiven. Or, two, we may be unable to identify with the darkness of sin seen in David, and so we question the need for anything dramatic or explicit.

Yesterday we looked at that encompassing statement, "We are convinced that (Christ) has died for all." Again, let it register solidly in your mind and heart: Since Christ has died for all, he has died for each, and that is the great solvent by which the love of God melts our hearts. This is the great proof that Jesus Christ loves me and loves you and loves all of us.

Now the "each" includes all of us. No matter the degree or depth or shade of our sin, Christ died for us. And he died that we might be forgiven.

If we don't know now, sooner or later we'll know—it will get through to us—that we have sinned, we are separated from God, and we do need to be reconciled to God. Nothing but the forgiveness of Christ will remedy that condition.

So while we may not have *an* experience of forgiveness (a one-time explicit occasion we can date and name), we must *experience* forgiveness. The awareness of the experience of forgiveness may come gradually, like the silent coming of the dawn of a winter day. We may not pinpoint the rising of the sun, but we know a new day has dawned. As we turn the calendar to make a new day in time, we need to turn the calendar in our relationship to Christ. This is it: I am forgiven!

Many of us need to do just that. Our experience has come gradually, but we need to nail it down, to make it explicit, even to verbalize it—"Christ forgives. I accept his forgiveness for myself. I am forgiven!"

Reflecting and Recording

Do whichever of the following seems appropriate to make explicit your claim of forgiveness:

Offer a prayer of confession, repentance, and acceptance of forgiveness.

***

Or, offer a prayer of thanksgiving for your previous, and your continuing, experience of forgiveness.

***

Write a note here, acknowledging your acceptance of forgiveness.

During the Day

Paraphrase John 3:16 by personalizing it, putting your name in the blanks and repeating it at flash prayer times during the day.

For God so loved _____that He gave His only
Son, that _____should not perish but have everlasting life.

DAY FOUR

Say Yes to Forgiveness by Forgiving Yourself

SOMEWHERE I READ A STORY ABOUT A NUN who had been raised in a very strict Catholic home. She had gone to a parochial school and all during those formative years of her life, she was terrified of the all-seeing eye of God. Her parents and her teachers had taught her that God was watching her all of the time. Unfortunately, they used the concept to frighten her into good behavior and to make sure that she never got out of line. When she became an adult, she was a very frightened and intimidated person.

One day she was talking with another nun, a very beautiful and happy person who had not grown up in a negative and punitive environment at all. She told this nun about her story and about how frightened she was of the eye of God that was watching her all of the time. She said, "Oh, my sister, you've got it wrong. God does see you all of the time, but do you know why? It is because he just can't take his eyes off of you!" How sensitive and wise was this other nun, and how clearly she understood the gospel.

Too many of us have grown up with a negative and punitive understanding of God. We may not be conscious of it, but we often picture God as a judge, a policeman, or a prosecuting attorney. Admittedly, there are scripture passages that suggest such an understanding. But the dominant witness of scripture is summarized by Jesus: "Fear not, little flock, for it is your Father's good pleasure to give you the kingdom" (Luke 12:32).

Because we do not really believe that sometimes and, instead, continue to believe that God is out to get us, we not only do not accept God's forgiveness, we find it terribly difficult, next to impossible, to forgive ourselves.

An unmarried college girl became pregnant and had an abortion. She was unable to believe in God's forgiveness or to forgive herself. She wrote to her minister, who replied: "The only real alternatives for you are to say yes or no to the forgiveness that God offers and that your family has so consistently given. By saying yes to this forgiveness and forgiving yourself, you honor God's love and the love of your family and friends and write end of chapter to all your yesterdays. The thing is finished, not to be reopened for any sort of renegotiation. Life for you begins now, and it begins with a clean start. It is as if this moment were the very moment of birth, and there's nothing on the record book for which you are held to account" (Sumner, p.62).

It is devastatingly painful to live with ourselves when we can't forgive ourselves for something we have done or something that has happened to us. Until we say yes to forgiveness by forgiving ourselves, our Christian Walk will be a hobbling one.

Reflecting and Recording

Have you had an experience in which someone wronged you painfully, yet you forgave them? In your imagination, get in touch with that experience.

***

Now ponder this question: If you cared enough for another person to forgive them, why do you not care enough for yourself to forgive yourself?

***

During the Day

Continue the flash prayer repetition of your personalized John 3:16.

DAY FIVE
Never Build a Case Against Yourself

THE ONGOING HAZARD EACH OF US FACES IN OUR CHRISTIAN WALK is a double one.

One side of it is to become so self-absorbed that our righteousness turns into self-righteousness. Do you know what I'm talking about? Persons can become so self-absorbed with their own righteousness that they allow it to turn into self-righteousness, and all of us know a few people like that.

But there is another hazard, and it is the opposite of that one. It is to slip into self-condemnation. I think it is easier to slip into self-condemnation than it is to slip into self-righteousness.

I am thinking of a story of a young minister serving his first congregation. He was still in seminary and was disenchanted with his work and also with himself. One day he was moaning about the state of affairs to a man in his congregation. The man had little formal education, but he was blunt and honest and possessed a great deal of native insight. As the young minister went on and on with his complaints, the wise old man suddenly made an impatient gesture and almost shouted, "Stop it! Stop all that defeatist, negative talk! Remember this, and remember it always: Never build a case against yourself!"

That is very good advice. We are always doing it, aren't we? We are always quick to slip into self-condemnation, into building a case against ourselves. We need to say yes to forgiveness by forgiving ourselves.

I heard another story that illustrates another facet of saying yes to forgiveness by forgiving yourself. I believe it is a story out of the life of Ruth Gordon, the actress. She had to overcome great difficulties to become an actress. Her parents were a liability to her. Her appearance was a disadvantage; she was not particularly attractive in a profession that considers glamour a primary asset. Her early training in drama was a discouragement. At the end of her junior year at the Academy of Dramatic Arts, the school told her not to come back. They said she had no acting talent.

But she went on to become a great actress. When she was in her eighties, she wrote her autobiography. In it, she gives her credo in these words: "Never face the facts unless you know how to forget them." I like that. How to forget is something we all need to learn. To keep painful memories alive, by refusing to forget, is like taking poison into our spirits.

And we are not likely to learn to forget, unless we learn to forgive. So, say yes to forgiveness by forgiving yourself.

Reflecting and Recording

Is there something you have done or something that has happened to you that you have not yet forgiven—not something that God has not forgiven, but that you have not forgiven. Name the experience here. Name persons and dates if possible, and describe it enough to relive it in your mind.

Now, in your imagination, see yourself before an altar in a church, or perhaps before the communion table. In your mind, look on the altar and see a small urn with a fire burning inside it. In your imagination, tear out what you have just written, crumple it in your hands, and put it into the fire.

As the fire consumes your crumpled paper, affirm to yourself that your painful experience is being burned up in the fire of God's forgetfulness. Repeat these words of God: "I am He who blots out your transgressions for my own sake, and I will not remember your sins" (Isaiah 43:25).

Affirm now to yourself: As God forgives and remembers no more, so I forgive and will remember no more. Then, in your imagination, leave the altar, determined to leave what you burned in the fire behind you forever.

***

During the Day

Copy the above word of God from Isaiah 43:25 on a piece of paper. Carry it with you for the next few days and take it out to read at the flash prayer points of your day.

DAY SIX

Saying Yes to Forgiveness Offers Freedom to the Other and Claims Freedom for Yourself

Judge not, and you will not be judged; condemn not, and you will not be condemned; forgive, and you will be forgiven; give, and it will be given to you; good measure, pressed down, shaken together, running over, will be put into your lap. For the measure you give will be the measure you get back.

—Luke 6:37-38

SAYING YES TO FORGIVENESS OFFERS FREEDOM to the one we forgive, and claims freedom for ourselves. There is a sense in which our enmity and estrangement from another holds both people in bondage. That is the reason Jesus said we have to forgive in order to be forgiven.

Let me underscore this point by addressing a particular issue—the issue of conflict in marriage. I don't believe that a family without conflict is a very healthy family. One writer has declared, "Show me a family that does not quarrel, and I will show you a family that will eventually fall apart." Well, I'm not sure we can be that dogmatic. Yet, statistics do show that most couples on the verge of divorce do not engage enough in open conflict; that is, they do not confront the issues with which they are dealing because they are afraid of conflict.

Some people think that the perfect marriage is one that is unmarred by conflict, one in which there are no arguments, no expression of differences, no sign of confrontation and estrangement. In fact, there are some who believe that you are truly Christian when you always have your feelings under control, never raise your voice, never lose your temper, and never take a person to task or do battle. That just isn't so. Jesus didn't teach it. Conflict is going to arise anywhere there is intimate relationship. The sign of health in a marriage and a home is not the absence of conflict. The sign of health in a marriage and a home is forgiveness.

You see, we can't live together intimately without hurting each other, but we can't keep on hurting each other and have the relationship survive without forgiveness. That's why I am telling you that saying yes to forgiveness offers freedom to the other person and claims freedom for yourself. If you remain estranged, if you remain separated from another, you hold both yourself and the other in bondage.

> Father William Scanlon was involved for many years working with runaway teenagers who gravitated to the Tenderloin District of San Francisco. Some of the stories which he related of adolescents who left home and family and ended up being exploited in the seamy life of drugs and prostitution make one's heart ache. One of his goals was to reunite the teenagers with their families. His efforts were not always successful, but there were wonderful times when teenagers went home with their families after moving moments of reconciliation. Sometimes the breakthrough occurred in the worship services which he conducted. He would ask people to join hands as they prayed together Our Lord's Prayer. He said there were tense moments as a parent would reach out a hand to a runaway son or daughter and the teenager would not respond. In certain situations, something else would begin to happen as the prayer started, "Our Father who art in Heaven, Hallowed be Thy name." Gradually the teenager's hand would open towards that of his or her parent. "Thy Kingdom come, Thy will be done on earth as it is in Heaven." Hands would then touch. "Give us this day our daily bread and forgive us our trespasses as we forgive those who trespass against us." Hands would grasp each other and tears would fill the eyes. As the prayer ended, parents and son or daughter, would be in each other's arms (Shelby, September 27, 1987).

Conflicts can be resolved as the grace of God works among us. We do not have to remain in bondage to the pain and resentment of unforgiveness. We can free others, and we can free ourselves, by saying yes to forgiveness.

Reflecting and Recording

Examine your relationships. Is there someone you need to forgive? If so, prayerfully devise a plan to actualize your forgiveness. The person you are thinking about may not be aware of your need to forgive. He or she may not have asked your forgiveness, but still you need to forgive because of how you feel and what you perceive. You may need to write a letter or call a person on the phone. Face to face sharing is the best, but that may not be possible. The important thing is for you to act, to take the initiative to forgive in order that you both may be free.

***

During the Day

Continue to use the Isaiah scripture passage at flash prayer points of your day.

DAY SEVEN

Our Clearest Witness

For if a man is in Christ he becomes a new person altogether—the past is finished and gone, everything has become fresh and new. All this is God's doing, for he has reconciled us to himself through Jesus Christ; and he has made us agents of the reconciliation. God was in Christ personally reconciling the world to himself—not counting their sins against them—and has commissioned us with the message of reconciliation.

—2 Corinthians 5:17-19, *PHILLIPS*

SOME YEARS AGO I WAS IN EAST GERMANY. Our host, a German pastor named Walter Friedman, took us to Görlitz, a beautiful, little town on the Polish border.

Despite its quaint beauty, Görlitz was a stark, depressing witness to the tragedy of war. After World War II, Russia took a huge part of Poland for herself, and as consolation, gave a small part of Germany to Poland. The line between the territory ran along the river that went through the heart of Görlitz. The city was divided at the river, one part of the city in Poland and the other part in Germany. Bridges across the river were destroyed. There was only one passage, one bridge from one part to the other. At that time, East German people could cross it only under the rarest of circumstances, for they were not allowed in Poland.

Persons who had been driven from their homes, now living on the German side, could look across the river and some of them could actually see their houses on the other side, houses they built with their own hands and paid for with their own money. They could look at them with longing, tear-filled eyes. They could see them, just across the river. It isn't a big river, but it was uncrossable and it kept them forever removed from what was once home. When we came to that river and that ominous barrier between Poland and East Germany, and my new friend told us the story of the division and the wrecked lives and homeless people, it brought to mind another story.

It was 1921, in southern Poland, following the devastation of another war. A Quaker nurse had given herself in selfless service to that war-torn land. She had spent herself in tireless love, and she died, having literally given her life away. The question arose, Where would she be buried? It was Roman Catholic territory and church law forbade any but baptized Catholics to be buried in the consecrated ground of a Catholic cemetery. It was also the only cemetery available and the nurse was deeply loved by all. Where would she be buried?

Finally, it was settled. The decision was made that she was to be buried just outside the cemetery fence. And so it was done. During the night, however, Polish peasants, faithful Roman Catholics, moved the fence so that the grave of their beloved nurse would be included inside the sacred ground.

Now that's what Christ does, and that's the task of Christians—to move fences, to tear down walls. "God was in Christ reconciling the world to himself, and has given us the ministry of reconciliation." I like the way Clarence Jordan paraphrases that great text—"God was in Christ, hugging the world to himself."

I am sure that is exactly what my friend Walter Friedman, and all of his Christian friends in East Germany, have been doing through the years, continuing the work of reconciliation. And now, with the fall of the Berlin Wall and the dissolving of the boundaries, how thrilled they must be with the newfound opportunity to express that ministry of forgiveness and reconciliation.

Saying yes to forgiveness is our clearest witness to the fact that we are Christian.

Reflecting and Recording

Look at your church and community. Are there points of estrangement where reconciliation is needed? Is there a way you can act and stimulate others to reconciling action?

***

Is there a specific ministry of your church that brings reconciliation? Could you initiate such a ministry?

***

Do you know persons who are estranged from each other for whom you might play an intermediary role for reconciliation?

***

Ponder this scripture as you commit yourself to a ministry of reconciliation.

> God was in Christ personally reconciling the world to himself—not counting their sins against them—and has commissioned us with the message of reconciliation. We are now Christ's ambassadors, as though God were appealing direct to you through us. As his personal representative we say, "Make your peace with God."   —2 Corinthians 5:19-20, *PHILLIPS*

During the Day

If you are in a group using this workbook together, make preparations for your meeting, and pray for those with whom you are sharing. Think of some person in the group, or some other person you know, who may be struggling with this matter of forgiveness. Call that person and assure them of your love and God's love.

WEEK FOUR

Group Meeting

Introduction

Paul advised the Philippians to "let your conversation be as it becometh the gospel" (Philippians 1:27, *KJV*). The Elizabethan word for *life* as used in the King James version is *conversation*, thus Paul's word to the Philippians. Life is found in communion with God and also in conversation with others. Most of us have yet to see the dynamic potential of the conversation that takes place in an intentional group such as this.

To listen is an act of love. When we listen in a way that makes a difference, we surrender ourselves to the other person, saying, "I will hear what you have to say and will receive you as I receive your words." When we speak in a way that makes a difference, we speak for the sake of others; thus we are contributing to the process of wholeness.

Speaking and listening with the sort of deep meaning that communicates life is not easy. This week our emphasis has been on forgiveness, the need to forgive, and the inability to do so. These things are not easy to talk about. Therefore, careful listening and responding to what we hear this week in the group meeting is very important. To really hear another person may be vital to the healing process that is going on in them.

As you speak and listen, you and others may receive the direction and strength to act in a relationship that needs the healing grace of forgiveness.

Sharing Together

1. Invite three or four willing persons to share their experience of actually receiving the forgiveness of Christ.

2. Spend eight to ten minutes discussing this statement: "Since Christ has died for all, he has died for each, and this is the great solvent by which the love of God melts our hearts."

3. Invite two or three persons to share an experience of forgiving another or an experience in which they truly forgave themselves.

4. Spend eight to ten minutes talking about *whether* and *why* it is easier to forgive another than oneself.

5. Discuss your church's ministry of reconciliation. Is that ministry taken seriously? What can you do to further the cause of reconciliation?

Praying Together

Corporate prayer is one of the great blessings of the Christian community. To affirm it is one thing, to experience it is another. To *experience* it we have to *experiment* with the possibility. Will you be a bit bolder now and experiment with the possibilities of corporate prayer by sharing more openly and intimately?

1. Let as many persons who will share a need for strength and guidance in forgiving another person. Or, if not a need in which they are personally involved, then the needs of others whom they know who are estranged for whom the group needs to pray.

2. Does any person have a need to forgive himself or herself and a willingness to share it with the group?

3. Now have a period of corporate prayer with as many people as are willing to offer verbal prayers.

At Home in the Daylight

DAY ONE

Children of the Light

Let no one deceive you with empty words, for it is because of these things that the wrath of God comes upon the sons of disobedience. Therefore do not associate with them, for once you were darkness, but now you are light in the Lord; walk as children of light (for the fruit of light is found in all that is good and right and true), and try to learn what is pleasing to the Lord. Take no part in the unfruitful works of darkness, but instead expose them. For it is a shame even to speak of the things that they do in secret; but when anything is exposed by the light it becomes visible, for anything that becomes visible is light. Therefore it is said, "Awake, O sleeper, and arise from the dead, and Christ shall give you light." Look carefully then how you walk, not as unwise men but as wise, making the most of the time, because the days are evil. Therefore do not be foolish, but understand what the will of the Lord is.

—Ephesians 5:6-17

MRS. ADAMS WAS PREPARING AN EARLY SUPPER for her twelve-year-old son so that he could get to football practice on time. Everything was ready when she discovered she was almost out of ketchup. She was thumping away at the end of the nearly empty bottle when the phone rang. You know how you do that—when the ketchup is scarce and it's hard to get out, you turn the bottle upside down and you thump on the bottom of it. Well, that's what she was doing when the phone rang.

"Would you get that?" she called to her son. Obligingly, he picked up the phone and the mother could hear him say to the caller, "She can't come to the phone right now. She's hitting the bottle." I hope whoever the caller was knew Mrs. Adams. Otherwise, you can imagine all the things that went through the caller's mind.

The story gets at our theme for this week. We are going to look at a number of aspects of our Christian Walk—daily kinds of things that really indicate who we are, things such as honesty and integrity, patience and perseverance.

The Christian Walk consists not so much of mastering the extreme demands, as in exercising the gifts so essential in everyday living. Paul puts it in a bold image, and the New English Bible translates verse eight of Ephesians 5 in this way: "For though you were once all darkness, now as Christians you are light. Live like men who are at home in daylight . . . ." The Revised Standard Version has that verse: ". . . for once you were darkness, but now you are light in the Lord; walk as children of light . . . ."

Our recurring image is there: "*walk*—as children of light." You may have noticed that, thus far, the scripture we have used to convey this image of walk has come primarily from Paul. But Paul is not alone. Though he had not heard Jesus say it, this passage offers strong evidence that long before the teachings we now have in the Gospels were written down, they were shared orally.

And this word of Paul is reminiscent of Jesus' word in John's Gospel. Jesus is aware of his coming death; the shadow of the cross is on his path. But he is conscious of his saving mission. "Now is this judgment of this world, now shall the ruler of this world be cast out; and I, when I am lifted up from the earth, will draw all men to myself" (John 12:31-32).

The crowd was puzzled at that. They said to Jesus in John 12:34, "We have heard from the law that the Christ remains forever. How can you say that the Son of man must be lifted up? Who is the Son of man?"

Now listen to Jesus' answer in verses 35 and 36: "The light is with you for a little longer. Walk while you have the light, lest the darkness overtake you; he who walks in the darkness does not know where he goes. While you have the light, believe in the light, that you may become sons of light."

The King James Version says, ". . . that you may be children of the light."

Do you see the connection? Paul is saying almost the same thing as Jesus: "For once you were darkness, but now you are light in the Lord; walk as children of the light."

To be in Christ is to be a child of light, and to believe in Christ is to be in him. To be in him is to walk in the light. So the image is provided for us by Jesus as well as by Paul. "Walk as children of light." "Live like men who are at home in daylight."

If we are going to walk as children of the light, we must be true to our deepest self. We dealt with this on **DAY SEVEN** of **WEEK TWO**, talking about the "freedom to be me." We underscore it here by focusing on personal integrity.

There is a proverb that says, "A righteous man who walks in his integrity—blessed are his sons after him" (Proverbs 20: 7).

I also think of Job here. He said, ". . . Till I die I will not put away my integrity from me" (Job 27:5). Imagine such a word in light of what had happened to Job. He had every reason not only to forget about his integrity, but to curse God and die. His wife even urged him to do so. He lost his extensive fortune and, shortly thereafter, he suffered the tragic death of his seven sons and three daughters. His health was broken, and he was driven to the edge of madness.

Yet he remained true to his deepest self; he kept his integrity. He is confident, always, in God. "But he knows the way that I take; when he has tried me, I shall come forth as gold" (Job 23:10). Now that's a dramatic test with which most of us could never identify. So maybe the point can best be made by focusing on something far from dramatic: *our personal feelings.*

If we are going to be true to our deepest self, we can't go on forever hiding our feelings. People are dying for want of other people who will be "at home in the daylight" where their feelings are concerned.

Most of us, men especially, are victims of what I call the "John Wayne Syndrome"—all strength, no weakness, keep the armor on, never risk vulnerability, keep your feelings to yourself. We fail to realize that what we present as strength and courage is often a veneer that hides our inability to share vulnerability as an essential part of love.

So, to be at home in the daylight means to be true to our deepest selves. And one expression of that is the willingness to show our feelings.

Reflecting and Recording

Examine the pattern of your life in terms of the way you express your feelings. Are you living in the dark by not letting others know how you truly feel?

***

During the Day

Pay attention to your relationships today. To what degree, how many times, and in what sort of circumstances do you find yourself holding back in expressing your deepest feelings?

DAY TWO

Manifest What You Are

You are the light of the world. A city set on a hill cannot be hid. Nor do men light a lamp and put it under a bushel, but on a stand, and it gives light to all in the house. Let your light so shine before men, that they may see your good works and give glory to your Father who is in heaven.   —Matthew 5:14-16

TO BE AT HOME IN THE DAYLIGHT, we must manifest what we are. That is what Jesus is telling us: "Let your light shine. . . ."

The slight difference between this and the previous exhortation to be true to our deepest self is that the first has to do with your integrity—your own wholeness. This one has the added dimension of witness. Not only must we be true to our deepest selves, we are to manifest what we are. We must see to it that what we are inside is reflected in our ordinary conduct, with every thought and deed a reflection of the light of Christ.

A Methodist minister, William Schwein, tells of a young woman who was a music major at the University of Indiana and an accomplished violinist. She grew up in a Jewish family but had not claimed her heritage of faith. One day she presented herself for membership in the Methodist Church in Bloomington, Indiana, and then she shared with Pastor Schwein her journey of faith that led to that decision. She recorded her experiences in a journal and she gave permission to Pastor Schwein to read and quote from it. This is what she wrote, in part:

Something very strange happened to me tonight. If I were to explain it to someone, I know I couldn't, so I will try to write it out on these pages. Perhaps it will pass, but it seems too emotionally exciting that I do not really want to lose it. Right after dinner I came upstairs to my room for the purpose of studying some music history for my exam tomorrow, but I never quite made it. That girl from down the hall, Nancy, passed my door, and I was determined to finally find out what it is that seems like a light around her.

The journal entry goes on to describe how she approached Nancy and asked her the secret of her inner glow. In the process, this neighbor down the hall told her about her faith in Jesus Christ and this was her reaction as recorded in the journal:

As Nancy spoke, I was filled with a strange feeling. I can't really describe it, but it was sort of like the anticipation I feel when something great is about to happen to me musically, only this was greater.

Some months later this brilliant student and musician accepted Christ and joined the Methodist Church. There was no button-holing and no intrusive "Are you saved?" but a simple sharing by another student of what Jesus Christ meant in her life. And by that quiet witness, another person found the joy of believing and the assurance of salvation through God's love in Christ. As Albert Outler puts it: "The world hears the Gospel when it sees it" (Schwein, January 11, 1987).

If we are going to live as those who are at home in the daylight, we must be true to our deepest self, and we must manifest what we are.

Reflecting and Recording

Reflect on the following questions, spending time with each before you even read the other.

Are there people you know well who do not know you are a Christian?

***

Are there values that you hold that are not known by the people with whom you work or socialize?

***

Is there something you feel strongly about that is only slightly known or not known at all by your spouse? Children? Closest friends?

***

Is there something that pains you that no one knows about, that you might even come to tears over if no one was looking?

***

Has anyone ever seen you cry?

***

What does your response to these questions say about your honesty and integrity?

During the Day

Pay attention to your relationships today. To what degree, how many times, and in what sort of circumstances do you find yourself holding back in expressing your deepest feelings?

DAY THREE
In Patience, Possess Your Soul

Nation shall rise against nation, and kingdom against kingdom: And great earthquakes shall be in divers places, and famines, and pestilences; and fearful sights and great signs shall there be from heaven. But before all these, they shall lay their hands on you, and persecute *you,* delivering *you* up to the synagogues, and into prisons, being brought before kings and rulers for my name's sake. And it shall turn to you for a testimony. Settle *it* therefore in your hearts, not to meditate before what ye shall answer: For I will give you a mouth and wisdom, which all your adversaries shall not be able to gainsay nor resist. And ye shall be betrayed both by parents, and brethren, and kinsfolks, and friends; and *some* of you shall they cause to be put to death. And ye shall be hated of all *men* for my name's sake. But there shall not a hair of your head perish. In your patience possess ye your souls. —Luke 21:10-19, *KJV*

I KNOW I HAVE ALREADY SAID that we are dealing this week with ordinary, everyday aspects of the Christian Walk. And I know that the above word of Jesus is not addressing ordinary times. Yet the last word is a word for all seasons: "In your patience possess ye your souls."

Other translations use the word endurance instead of patience—"By your endurance you will gain your lives." Or standing firm—"By standing firm you will win your souls" (*PHILLIPS*). All of which is to simply expand our understanding of patience.

If patience can function to save us in the tumultuous times of life, how much will it sustain, flavor, and give meaning to our ordinary day to day living? It is a characteristic of the Christian Walk, and it is essential if we are to be at home in the daylight. Consider the way patience serves our life and colors our Christian Walk.

For one thing, being patient recognizes that we are not in control. And we need that discipline don't we? We need the discipline of *waiting,* of knowing that we are not in control.

Several elderly church members were being asked to what they contributed their longevity. "Mabel, why do you think God has permitted you to reach the age of ninety-two?" one wealthy old woman was asked.

Without hesitation, she replied, "To test the patience of my relatives."

And have you heard this commentary? "Men will wait three hours for the fish to bite, and won't wait 15 minutes for their wives to get dressed."

Ezekiel expresses it beautifully. He pictures God taking a sprig, the topmost growing point of a great cedar, and planting it in another land. It is an allegory of the Jews returning from exile into Palestine and starting their lives over again. God takes just a sprig, the smallest of branches on the tree. But in time, the allegory says, it grows into a noble cedar under which all the animals of the earth find shade, and in whose branches all the birds of the air can build their nest. It began as a little sprig and grew to a noble cedar, and it is all God's doing. And that's the point: It is all God's doing.

The passage ends with a declaration of who is in charge: ". . . I the Lord bring low the high tree, and make high the low tree . . . . I the Lord have spoken and I will do it" (Ezekiel 17:24).

Isn't this what Jesus was saying in his two little parables about farmers sowing seed? It's not something that we do; it's not something that we produce. One line tells the whole story: "The earth produces of itself." It is out of our hands; it is the Lord's doing. Being patient recognizes that we are not in control.

Reflecting and Recording

Spend a few minutes moving in your mind through the last 24 hours—beginning with the time you got out of bed yesterday. Consciously register everything that happened, everything you did. How much did you control? How important was what you had control over? What lessons were there in patience?

***

During the Day

As you move through this day, note the times you verge on impatience. Seek to be patient, but also ask what lesson is there in your impatience.

DAY FOUR
The Weight of Glory

I tell you, my friends, do not fear those who kill the body, and after that have no more that they can do. But I will warn you whom to fear: fear him who, after he has killed, has power to cast into hell; yes, I tell you, fear him! Are not five sparrows sold for two pennies? And not one of them is forgotten before God. Why, even the hairs of your head are all numbered. Fear not; you are of more value than many sparrows.
—Luke 12:4-7, *RSV*

When I look at thy heavens, the work of thy fingers, the moon and the stars which thou hast established; what is man that thou art mindful of him, and the son of man that thou dost care for him? Yet thou hast made him little less than God, and dost crown him with glory and honor.   —Psalm 8:3-5

TO PRACTICE PATIENCE is to show that we value the other person. Jesus and the psalmist placarded the value of persons before us: "the hairs on our head are numbered"; we are "a little lower than the angels." Maybe you have seen that desk placard and bumper sticker, "Be patient with me; God is not finished with me yet." It is a plea we might all make.

When we realize that God is not finished with us, we realize that, likewise, God is not finished with those around us. So, as surely as we want patience for ourselves, we must give patience to others. When we are patient with another person, we are saying to that person, "I value you, you are important. I am willing to spend my time to give you my attention."

One of C. S. Lewis's basic beliefs was that we are all children of the king, and have a right, as such, to go on a journey to and with him. The king, and eternal life with him, is our destination and our journey. In talking about this, Katherine Lindskoog coined the phrase, "The right of destination." I think that is a marvelous phrase, the right of destination.

C. S. Lewis and others have taught theology through fairy tale. Consider the first few sentences of George McDonald's *The Princess and The Goblin*.

"There was once a little princess who—"
"But, Mr. Author, why do you always write about princesses?"
"Because every little girl is a princess."
"You will make them vain if you tell them that."
"Not if they understand what I mean."
"Then what do you mean?"
"What do you mean by a princess?"
"The daughter of a king."
"Very well, then every little girl is a princess . . . ."

This is also C. S. Lewis's concept of man. It is my concept, and I believe, the Bible's. We are all princes and princesses, the sons and daughters of a king. Although our ultimate destination may be the same, the journey is so different for each of us. Some of us are burdened with almost unbearable cares and sorrows, while others fly through life in a breeze. Some of us pretty much fulfill our potential, while others waste it and fall short of the mark any loving king would will for his princes and princesses.

Lewis was especially cognizant of our obligation to help one another fulfill that potential. In his book *The Weight of Glory,* he spoke of the glory of one's neighbor; and the weight was our call to help the neighbor reach that glory. Even the dullest and most uninteresting person may some day become a creature we will greatly admire, "or else a horror and a corruption such as is seen only in a nightmare." Lewis concludes, "All day long we are, in some degree, helping each other to one or the other of these destinations."

It is a burden, but a joyful opportunity—to bear the weight of glory for others. And patience is the primary expression of our willingness to bear that weight.

Reflecting and Recording

Look through the following *categories* (I wish I had a better word) of persons. By as many as you wish, place the name of a person for whom you feel *the weight of glory,* to whom you need to show value by patience.

Parent—

Children—

Spouse—

Friend—

Associate at work—

Boisterous, loud, seeking attention—

Quiet, insecure, intimidated—

Divorced, needing affirmation—

The latter three categories are suggestive; think of others you might add. Offer a prayer for these persons, and a prayer for yourself to be patient with them.

During the Day

Again, as you move through this day, note the times you verge on impatience. Seek to be patient, but also ask what lesson is there in your impatience.

DAY FIVE
Keeping Our Values Clear

WE'VE BEEN THINKING ABOUT PATIENCE. Let's look now at gratitude. All of life is a gift and not to realize it is a slap in the face of God.

The psalmist expressed it, "The earth is the Lord's and the fulness thereof, the world and those who dwell therein . . . " (Psalm 24:1).

Since this is a workbook on the Christian Walk, we are going to look at gratitude from the perspective of how it enhances our walk and how it witnesses to the fact that "we walk in the light." From that vantage point, being grateful keeps our values clear.

Loren Eiseley, in his book *All The Strange Hours,* talks about the time when he inhabited a ghost world. It was back in 1948. He and his wife were living in suburban Philadelphia. He was in his first year as a faculty member at the University of Pennsylvania. It was a cold damp fall and he had always been susceptible to respiratory ailments.

> One night, after what had seemed a mild cold, I awoke in the dark conscious that I was running a fever and babbling a lecture to some unseen audience. Slowly, as my consciousness steadied, I grew aware of something strange. Outside, lightning bolts sporadically split the dark. I could see through the bedroom window a torrential rain in progress. After each stroke of lightning I waited for the following thunder. There was none. I was deaf . . . . I was alone with that knowledge in the dark (Eiseley, p. 178).

He woke his wife and asked her to speak. Her lips moved, but he could not hear her voice. It was the beginning of a long, frightening winter. His mother had been stone-deaf all her life, and in the back of his mind, there had been that subconscious worry that maybe he would inherit the problem. His fear had become fact. What would happen to his teaching career? He could lecture, but he couldn't hear the questions students asked. He was referred from one specialist to another as he sought help.

It was a nightmare, living in a ghost world. With people around him laughing and chatting, but him not hearing them, they were like ghosts, with gesticulating hands and moving lips, but no other life, at least for Eiseley. The sounds of trains, rolling baggage trucks, the ordinary noises of life did not exist for him.

During the winter, the situation didn't change. But then, on a late March evening, he got the first indication that his hearing would return. He was seated in the kitchen, waiting for supper, when suddenly he became aware of a soft, sputtering purr that seemed to come from somewhere near the stove. It was the gas flame. He jumped to his feet and asked his wife if she heard it. He was almost delirious with joy.

The return of his hearing was a gradual process. In his book, he talks about walking out onto their little balcony.

> The air was soft. Clear as the voices of my childhood, the spring peepers sounded in the trees above the brook. I listened as though I could never have enough. "I ought to write something about this and the kettle," I said to my wife. "But mostly the kettle. I mean that little flame and how it purred. People don't appreciate things like that, they never do till they are gone. I turn it on now sometimes when you're away, just for company" (Eiseley, p. 184).

It is a dramatic witness. The sound of a gas flame is no big thing—unless you can't hear it! To live in appreciation for all the gifts of life and deliberately express gratitude keeps our values clear.

Reflecting and Recording

Make a list of the things you take for granted such as the availability of water and the access to medical care.

_____

_____

_____

_____

_____

Now, add to that what may be considered unessential things, such as the sound of laughter, singing birds, wind in the trees, and so forth.

_____

_____

_____

_____

Ponder this question: If you were intentional in your gratitude for the above things, would it affect your values?

***

During the Day

Offer flash prayers of gratitude for the things that you experience today, and the persons in your life you take for granted.

DAY SIX

A Clear Expression of Our Dependency on God

> For who sees anything different in you? What have you that you did not receive? If then you received it, why do you boast as if it were not a gift?
>
> —1 Corinthians 4:7

NOT ONLY DOES BEING GRATEFUL KEEP OUR VALUES CLEAR, it is one of the clearest expressions of our dependency on God. Paul expressed it so clearly in the above passage. Is there anything we have that is important and essential to life that we did not receive?

It ties back to the point that we looked at on **DAY THREE**: Patience reminds us of who is in control.

Isn't it amazing? Despite everything that has happened to prove otherwise, we keep falling back into the snare of thinking we are in control. One dark day in October, 1987, the stock market tumbles—and we still think we are independent and in control.

A doctor comes out of his examination room to announce to a waiting husband, "As we suspected, your wife has cancer"—and we think we are independent and in control.

We wage our hot and our cold wars. We use all our human powers to plot the future of a world divided by an Iron Curtain and a Berlin Wall, and to the utter surprise of the whole world, the wall is battered down and the curtain begins to rise—and we think we are independent and in control.

Doctors pronounce at least a 50% deficiency of sight in a little boy, and there is no treatment for his malady, no chance for his overcoming the limitation, and two years later that same little boy, with no medical treatment, has 20/40 vision—and we think we are independent and in control.

Gratitude, informed and genuine gratitude, is one of the clearest expressions of our dependency on God.

I heard about a woman who captured this truth in this way. She was talking about giving thanks at meals, and she said, "We say grace every night around here because we think it's a good idea to give up our egos to God."

Well it is a good idea, a very good idea, to give up our egos and acknowledge our dependence by being grateful.

There is a great thanksgiving hymn that most of us know, "Now Thank We All Our God." It was written by a pastor named Martin Rinkart after the village in which he served had been almost destroyed. In 1637, first a plague and then a famine swept across the town. In that one year, over eight thousand persons perished. It almost destroyed a heroic people, but a few survived, and one of them was the pastor who wrote this hymn.

At first, it was used as a prayer for his own family at mealtime. Since that time, it has been used throughout the world. It has been sung at the dedication of great cathedrals and in German churches on New Year's Eve, and it occupies a prominent place in many hymnbooks.

Do you know why? Because through those words, people everywhere have learned to identify with the grace that is sufficient for every need.

> Now thank we all our God,
> With heart and hands and voices,
> Who wondrous things has done,
> In whom this world rejoices;
> Who from our mothers' arms
> Has blessed us on our way
> With countless gifts of love,
> And still is ours today.

Squeezed from a life that was stripped of so much, this pastor found the grace of God sufficient for his every need. And being grateful is one of the clearest expressions of our dependency upon God.

Reflecting and Recording

Write a prayer of thanksgiving, expressing your dependency on God, recognizing God's gifts, and acknowledging what you treasure.

During the Day

Again, today offer flash prayers of gratitude for the things that you experience today and the persons in your life you may take for granted.

DAY SEVEN

Hanging In When the Odds Are Against Us

THE CHRISTIAN WALK IS NOT A SMOOTH ONE. It is often rough and demanding. So we have to hang in there when the odds are against us and there is no apparent reason for hope. The word for that is perseverance.

In closing his letter to the Ephesians, Paul minces no words in his warning. According to Paul, as Christians, we are involved in warfare. It is not just a battle with the weakness of our flesh or with limitations of our mortality. And it is not solely the war that is raging inside us that he talked about in Romans 7 and 8—"For the good that I would I do not, and the evil that I would not, that I do. O wretched man that I am. Who will deliver me from this body doomed to death."

It is not a solitary, personal battle such as that. It is a battle with powers beyond ourselves. "For we are not contending against flesh and blood, but against the principalities, against the powers, against the world rulers of this present darkness, against the spiritual hosts of wickedness in the heavenly places" (Ephesians 6:12).

Against all of that, Paul says, "Be strong in the Lord and in the strength of his might" (Ephesians 6:10). Then in verse 11, he uses the military metaphors of girding ourselves for battle, "Put on the whole armor of God, that you may be able to stand against the wiles of the Devil." Then he names all those implements of military armor. These become the spiritual armor against principalities and powers of evil. Then he says, "Pray at all times in the Spirit, with all prayer and supplication. To that end keep alert with all perseverance, making supplication for all the saints . . ." (Ephesians 6:18). There is the word—perseverance.

Now here is our problem: Most of us want to get to the Promised Land without going through the wilderness. Isn't that the way it is?

When we talk about perseverance, we are talking about burning the midnight oil. We are talking about painful study, gritty grind, energy-draining toil and weariness. We're talking about desperate struggle. It doesn't happen otherwise. But our problem is that we want the end, but we do not want the inevitable preliminaries. We would have the success without the grind and toil and daily discipline, but that is simply impossible.

I think of the life of a recovering alcoholic. Now here are some people who can witness to perseverance. They know that they must persevere in those twelve steps, and they must take it a day at a time.

But there are other areas. How many marriages could be saved by perseverance? How many persons could be won to Christ if we would persevere in our witness? How many children would come back home from the far country if we would persevere in our love?

I talked to a fellow a few weeks ago, a young man who would almost fit the typical Yuppie stereotype. But it has only been lately that he fits that stereotype. He spent five years in the far country of drugs, sexual promiscuity, and wasted living. Do you know what he said to me about his father? "He didn't give up on me." And then he added, "Neither did God."

Those two things go together. They always do. It may be that our not giving up on a person is the only witness that person will have that God doesn't give up either.

Reflecting and Recording

Have you had someone who made a difference in your life by being patient with you, and persevering? Name that person here.

_____

Spend a minute or two thinking about that person. What was he or she like? What did he or she do for you? How did you feel?

***

Are there persons and situations in which you are presently involved that you are tempted to give up on? Name them here.

_____

_____

_____

Think now of the who didn't give up on you. What would he or she do in the above cases?

***

Pray now that God will give you the strength to persevere a little longer.

During the Day

If the person you named above who was patient and persevered with you is alive, call him or her on the phone or write a letter expressing your gratitude.

If you know a person who is having a hard time persevering in a tough situation, call or write him or her with a word of encouragement.

If you are studying this workbook with a group, make plans for your meeting, and pray for those who are sharing with you.

WEEK FIVE

Group Meeting

Introduction

John Wesley called on Christians to use all the "means of grace" available for their Christian Walk, their growth in Christlikeness. Along with the ones that we normally think of—prayer, scripture, study, worship, holy communion—Wesley named Christian conferencing. By it, he meant intentional Christian conversation, talking about spiritual matters, and sharing our Christian Walk.

These group sessions provide practice in the art of Christian conferencing. As you share together in the "safe" setting of a group of mutually-committed persons, you are being equipped to share in less safe relationships. Keep that in mind as you share in this session and as you continue your weekly gatherings.

Sharing Together

1. You have finished five weeks of this workbook journey. Spend a few minutes talking about the experience in general terms. What is giving you difficulty? What is providing the most meaning?

2. Spend eight to ten minutes discussing the "John Wayne syndrome." Keep your discussion centered on personal experience.

3. Ask the group members to turn in their workbooks to the *Reflecting and Recording* section of **WEEK FIVE**. Spend fifteen minutes discussing your feelings and responses to the series of questions there, focusing on the last one: "What do your responses to these questions say about your honesty and integrity?"

4. Invite two or three persons to share their experience of a time when a person exercised great patience and perseverance with them, and the difference that made in their life.

5. Close your discussion time by inviting anyone who wishes to do so to raise questions or discuss issues of concern in their response to this week's content.

Praying Together

Spontaneous conversational prayer—persons offering brief sentences—is a powerful dynamic in our group life. One person may offer a sentence or two now, and then again after two or three others have prayed. One person's prayer may suggest another. Don't try to say everything in your one prayer. Pray pointedly, knowing you can pray again during this time of prayer. This way you can be spontaneous and not strain to make sure you have "covered all the bases."

1. Invite those who wish to do so to share a current situation with which they are having to persevere. Let two or three others in the group offer sentence prayers in response to this sharing.

2. Invite two or three persons to share the prayers of thanksgiving they wrote on **DAY SIX**.

3. Close now by giving persons the opportunity to share specific prayer requests, and then spend a brief time in spontaneous conversational prayer.

4. Turn the pictures upside down so that each person can take one and pray daily for that person during the upcoming week.

WEEK SIX
A Fragrant Offering

DAY ONE

"And Walk in Love"

A TEACHER SENT HOME A REPORT CARD with this notation to the parents. "Alvin excels in initiative, group integration, responsiveness, and activity participation. Now if he would only learn to read and write!"

We chuckle, but there is a serious point here. We have excelled in almost every way imaginable as human beings except in the one way that matters most. We have not learned to love.

The most distinctive characteristic of our Christian Walk and our greatest need is love. Paul gives us a beautiful description in Ephesians. He calls us to the Christian Walk and he does it in an unforgettable way.

> Therefore be imitators of God, as beloved children. And walk in love, as Christ loved us and gave himself up for us, a fragrant offering and sacrifice to God.
> —Ephesians 5:1-2

That is the image I would like to lodge in your mind—living a life of love, love that was expressed in its ultimate meaning in Christ's giving of himself for us. Paul called that "a fragrant offering." What we are calling for, then, as we remind ourselves to walk in love, is for each one of us to become "a fragrant offering" on behalf of others.

I devoted a good part of the early sections of this workbook to the gospel principle that is the overarching one for our Christian Walk: We are persons in Christ. That means we are *in* love. John wrote:

> Beloved, let us love one another; for love is of God, and he who loves is born of God and knows God. He who does not love does not know God; for God is love. In this the love of God was made manifest among us, that God sent his only Son into the world, so that we might live through him. In this is love, not that we loved God but that he loved us and sent his Son to be the expiation for our sins. Beloved, if God so loved us, we also ought to love one another. No man has ever seen God; if we love one another, God abides in us and his love is perfected in us.
> —1 John 4:7-12

In essence, John is saying, God sent Jesus into the world to be the ultimate expression of himself, an expression of love. And for what purpose? That we might live through him.

And what is the sign that we live through him? "Beloved, if God so loved us, we also ought to love one another" (vs. 11). And then there is that remarkable word in verse 12: "No man has ever seen God; if we love one another, God abides in us and his love is perfected in us."

I have heard the story of a reporter visiting a small community of Roman Catholic lay workers in northern California that takes in and cares for babies who are dying of AIDS. The reporter was talking with a woman who was holding a pathetically small baby girl that was obviously very ill and the reporter asked about the baby.

The woman said, "Her mother was a prostitute, a heroin addict, and she didn't want a baby. The baby was born addicted to heroin and infected with AIDS." Then she added, "The baby will probably die soon."

"Then why do you do this," asked the reporter. "I mean, why did you bring her up here to your community if she is going to die very shortly?"

The woman responded without hesitation, "So she will know life in all its fullness."

The reporter was obviously taken aback by this. He was incredulous. With a tone of cynicism in his voice, he said, "How can this pitiful baby know life in its fullness?"

And the caring shepherd of this baby said, "She will know that there are people in this world who love her."

That is what everybody needs to know, isn't it? And those who are on the Christian Walk must be the channels of that love.

Reflecting and Recording

Of all the persons you know, who best personifies the description "a fragrant offering?" Name that person here and describe him or her in a paragraph, naming his or her primary characteristics.

Would you say that person is Christlike?

***

Is there anything about that person that suggests *sacrificial love*?

***

Offer a prayer of thanksgiving for that person.

During the Day

If the person you described above is alive, write a note or make a phone call to tell him or her about this exercise. If the person is not living, tell someone else today about this exercise and about that person you know who personifies "a fragrant offering."

DAY TWO
Loving Expresses Itself in Understanding

> Beloved, let us love one another; for love is of God, and he who loves is born of God and knows God. He who does not love does not know God; for God is love. In this the love of God was made manifest among us, that God sent his only Son into the world, so that we might live through him. In this is love, not that we loved God but that he loved us and sent his Son to be the expiation of our sins.
> —1 John 4:7-10

TO WALK IN LOVE AS CHRISTIANS—to be the fragrant offering to others that Christ would have us be—is to practice a love that expresses itself in understanding, but hangs tough.

Now, we all needs someone who understands us. I don't know any philosopher who understands the meaning of being human and the meaning of human relationship as well as Martin Buber. He says that "secretly and bashfully, we watch for a *Yes* which allows us to *be*, and which can come to us only from one person to another." To understand another is to say yes to the other—affirming that person in his or her very being.

I do not know *why* it is, but I do know that it is: our *being*, our living as full human beings is really dependent upon our being accepted by others. That acceptance requires understanding and trust. Indeed, such acceptance is one of the surest experiences of God's presence in our lives. John expressed it pungently: "No man has ever seen God; if we love one another, God abides in us, and his love is perfected in us" (Ephesians 4:12).

Jim Moore tells the story of a little boy who was diagnosed as having a terminal illness. One wonders why, but the little boy was told the situation and that he would soon die. The trauma was so great, he retreated fearfully into a cocoon of total silence. No one, not doctors or nurses or even his parents, could get through to him. No one could penetrate the wall of silence and the boy refused to speak to anyone. The only way he would communicate was through drawings he sketched and colored on a legal pad.

One drawing showed a beautiful cottage set off to the side of the paper. Above the cottage, the sun was shining brightly. Surrounding the cottage was a beautiful lawn with flowers and trees. On the lawn in front of the cottage there was a family of four, a mother, a father and two children. In the center of the paper, there was a tiny figure standing there all alone and facing a large army tank that was bearing down upon him about to run him down. Obviously, the tiny figure represented the dying child who saw himself as so small, so vulnerable, and so helpless before the gigantic force about to destroy him.

Some ministerial students were brought in and told about the little boy's illness and his self-imposed silence. Then they were shown the picture of the boy and the tank and were asked how they would help this child. How would they try and break through the silence and get him to talk again, to talk about his feelings and fears? How would they offer him faith and comfort and hope? It was suggested to the students that the approach would be for them to try to communicate through this drawing by adding something to the picture.

One by one, the seminarians came forward to try. One drew a picture of a man holding a stop sign in front of the tank, but it didn't get anywhere with the little boy. Others made their attempt as well, but nothing worked.

Finally, there was a breakthrough. One seminarian drew the picture that knocked down the wall of silence, causing the boy to speak and to eventually pour out all his pent-up feelings to that seminarian.

What was the picture? A person was added to the picture and the person was doing a very simple thing. Just holding the hand of the little boy who was facing that huge tank. The presence of a supportive friend made all the difference. It enabled the little boy to face his fears and deal with his problems and talk about them with courage and hope (Moore, July 8, 1989).

Consider Buber's word again—"Secretly and bashfully, we watch for a *Yes* which allows us to *be*, and which can come to us only from one person to another." Love that expresses itself in understanding is that *Yes*.

Reflecting and Recording

Looking back over your life, who is the one person (other than your spouse or parents) who has been the *Yes* for you through love that expressed itself in understanding? Name and describe that person here.

Name a person that you may have been the *Yes* to. Be honest. It is not a matter of unholy pride to acknowledge the ministry you may have provided another. So, overcome your reservations and write the name here. _____

Now it could be that you have expressed understanding love that has been far more meaningful to someone than you will ever know. Maybe one of the joys of heaven will be people telling us what our love meant to them. The question is, What does our struggle in naming someone for whom our love has made a significant difference tell us about our love?

***

During the Day

If the person you described as your *Yes* is living, write a note or make a phone call, and express *your gratitude*. Again, if he or she is not living, tell someone else the story.

DAY THREE
Love Hangs Tough

I REPEAT: TO WALK IN LOVE AS CHRISTIANS—to be the fragrant offering to others Christ would have us be—is to practice a love that expresses itself in understanding, but hangs tough.

If we know any scriptures at all that are related to love, we are likely to know two. One is John 3:16: "For God so loved the world that he gave his only son, that whoever believes in him should not perish but have eternal life." That is tough demanding, serious business. God's love is deep enough that God is willing to die for us. And the second scripture we probably know that is related to love is 1 Corinthians 13. In verse 7 of that marvelous hymn of love, Paul says, "Love bears all things, believes all things, hopes all things, endures all things."

Love hangs tough. It hangs tough because it bears all things, believes all things, hopes all things, and endures all things.

Jane Isbell Haynes, a member of the congregation I serve, is a published William Faulkner scholar. I have confessed to her often that I have difficulty reading Faulkner. Now and then, she will tell me as she leaves church on Sunday morning that my sermon had a Faulkner theme. I can understand that because Faulkner was grounded in biblical themes.

One of Faulkner's finest novels is *The Sound & the Fury,* a novel that chronicles the moral disintegration and decay of a Southern family named Compson. One character stands like a towering rock of strength in the midst of the waste, decadence, and conflict. Her name is Dilsey, and she is the servant. Her presence is a bright constant light in the growing darkness. She watches in love all that is going on in the family and often weeps as she works. She prays and agonizes in silence as she tries to help the family, through more than one generation of demise. In listing the characters in the novel, Faulkner includes a brief description of each. For Dilsey, and the other blacks in the story, there were but two words: "They endured."

How? Why? I believe that Dilsey knew she was loved by God, and that knowledge was deep and strong. That is why she gave so much love. And because she loved, she endured.

Love hangs tough because it wills the well-being and the wholeness of the person loved. Love hangs tough because love has integrity and cannot abide sham and pretense.

Reinhold Niebuhr once observed that "it is difficult to be honest and human at the same time." Well, it is, but love is honest and human—it hangs tough, because it will not settle for deception and pretense.

It hangs tough because what it seeks is character. It seems as though we've reached a place in our day that we have changed our vocabulary and our thinking in order to accommodate ourselves to the lowest moral expectations. A sense of moral standards and responsibility and accountability have almost completely disappeared from our human scene. But that's the reason love hangs tough. It seeks to build and preserve character.

Because it hangs tough, sometimes it has to do the painful thing. It may have to cut off financial support to a son or daughter to bring that son or daughter to a place of maturity. It may have to hang tough to the point of leaving a daughter in jail for a week to hopefully bring her to her senses. That happened with a couple in our church a few weeks ago. They knew the meaning, but also the pain of tough love. It may have to speak the painful truth in order to save a person from living a lie and betraying himself or herself.

So, because it hangs tough, love sometimes has to do the painful thing.

Yet, we need to remember this: When love doesn't hang tough, all sorts of destructive things happen. For example, marriage vows are trivialized, and love and commitment become empty words. Or persons who have great promise are never called to maturity and fulfillment because they are betrayed by a love that has no demanding edge to it.

So while Christian love expresses itself in understanding, it hangs tough.

Reflecting and Recording

Spend some time pondering this question: "How many times do we take the Prodigal Son home again?"

***

In what situations and with what persons do you need to express tough love?

***

During the Day

Call someone you know who is having to exercise tough love and encourage that person.

DAY FOUR
Generosity of Self

ONE OF THE MOST EFFECTIVE AND COLORFUL CONGRESSMEN to ever go to Washington was a crusty old gentleman from Texas named Sam Rayburn. He served Congress for over fifty years and during the last ten of those years, he was Speaker of the House. But the real greatness of Sam Rayburn was not in the public positions he held. It was in his common touch.

One day he heard that the teenage daughter of a Washington reporter had died. Early the next morning, he went over to the reporter's house and knocked on the door. "I just came by to see what I could do to help," he said.

The reporter was obviously touched. "Well, thank you, Mr. Speaker, but I don't think there is anything you can do. We're handling all the arrangements."

Rayburn said to him, "Let me ask you—have you had your coffee yet this morning?" When the reporter said that he had not, Mr. Sam said "Well, I'll make it for you."

Without giving the fellow time to object, Rayburn went into the house and began to make coffee in the kitchen. The reporter was taken aback. "Mr. Speaker," he said, "I thought you were having breakfast at the White House with the President this morning."

Mr. Rayburn responded, "Well, I was, but I called the President and told him I had a friend who was having some trouble, and that I wouldn't be in today."

The story suggests a much needed dimension of love and our Christian Walk: generosity of self.

Our Christian Walk is one of generosity because we know that all of life is gift. That is what Paul is saying when he says, "For who sees anything different in you? What have you that you did not receive? If then you received it, why do you boast as if it were not a gift?" (1 Corinthians 4:7).

I like Dennis the Menace. In one cartoon, Mrs. Wilson had told Dennis that Mr. Wilson used to be just like Dennis. Later, Dennis explains that to his friend: "He got dirty an' had flights and swiped cookies—an' busted things, and told fibs, and hated baths—and teased girls!" Dennis's friend replies, "Gee! He sounds like a reg'lar fella! I wonder where he went wrong!"

Where did Mr. Wilson go wrong? Where do we go wrong? When did we lose our childlike trust and turn into cynics? When did we lose the acceptance of life as grace and turn into dog-eat-dog achievers? When did we cease seeing life as a gift and decide that we had to take it by storm? Are you living your life, are you spending your life, as though it were gift?

Reflecting and Recording

One way to get a reading on how generous we are with our self is to look at how we react to interruptions. Look back over the last five days and list five or six interruptions. Just name a person or time it happened—enough to label the incident as an interruption. Make the list without too much thought, except that it *was* an interruption.

_____

_____

_____

_____

_____

_____

Now go back and look at each interruption. Write down your reactions to each of them—what you did, what you said, how you felt. What does the exercise say about your generosity of self?

***

During the Day

Before you react to an interruption or any call that seems to impose itself on you today, ask if a response of generosity is in order.

DAY FIVE

Generosity of Money

As for the rich in this world, charge them not to be haughty, nor to set their hopes on uncertain riches but on God who richly furnishes us with everything to enjoy. They are to do good, to be rich in good deeds, liberal and generous, thus laying up for themselves a good foundation for the future, so that they may take hold of the life which is life indeed.   —1 Timothy 6:17-19

MANY OF YOU WILL KNOW THE NAMES of Bunker, Lamar, and Herbert Hunt. They were the Texas brothers who were once among the wealthiest people in the world.

Some years ago, they tried to corner the world's silver market. That effort backfired on them, and in 1986, they went into bankruptcy. Newspapers across the nation ran stories about the Hunts' flagship corporation, one of the largest, privately-owned oil companies in the world. In one story, the focus was on the financial reserves of this famous American family—a family of vast wealth. At one point, Bunker Hunt made an observation about his own father: "My Dad really never cared about money, but it just sort of seemed the way they kept score."

What a tragedy—to be using money, and the accumulation of it, as merely a way to keep score. How we feel about money and how we use it says much about who we are. But more than that, it tells the story of *whose* we are.

A Methodist preacher in Columbus, Ohio, was visiting one of the community's most wealthy and influential men. As they were talking about the problems of the world and what a Christian's response should be, the man rose from his desk and walked to the windows of his impressive office with its commanding view of the city. He gazed out of the window for a time, then turned and said to the preacher, "You know, Barry, I've kind of got it figured out that God still ask us two questions when we knock on the gate of heaven. I really mean this. First, he's going to ask, "What have you done with all you had?" Now, that's an easy one to answer, we all know what we've done with what we had. The second question, though, is a tougher one, for God is then going to ask, "Who did you do it for?"

You see, how we use our money tells much about who we are, but, more importantly, it tells whose we are.

Listen again to what Paul was saying to Timothy. "They are to do good, to be rich in good deeds, liberal and generous." So, no matter how much money we have, we are on common ground before the Lord because he will judge us on the basis of how we use what we have.

And this clear and challenging word comes from the diary of a missionary: "He is no fool who gives up that which he cannot keep, in order to gain that which he cannot lose."

Jesus said, "Where your treasure is, there your heart will be, also."

You can lose your treasure, many people have. And if your treasure is in the wrong place, you will lose your soul as well. But if your treasure is in the right place, even though you lose it, your soul will be saved for eternity.

Reflecting and Recording

Reflect on these questions: What are you doing with what you have? And who are you doing it for?

***

During the Day

Look for a chance today, even a small one, to use money in an unselfish way.

DAY SIX
The Ministry of Making Many Rich

> We put no obstacle in any one's way, so that no fault may be found with our ministry, but as servants of God we commend ourselves in every way: through great endurance, in afflictions, hardships, calamities, beatings, imprisonments, tumults, labors, watching, hunger; by purity, knowledge, forbearance, kindness, the Holy Spirit, genuine love, truthful speech, and the power of God; with the weapons of righteousness for the right hand and for the left; in honor and dishonor, in ill repute and good repute. We are treated as impostors, and yet are true; as unknown, and yet well known; as dying, and behold we live; as punished, and yet not killed; as sorrowful, yet always rejoicing; as poor, yet making many rich; as having nothing, and yet possessing everything.
>
> —2 Corinthians 6:3-10

THIS SCRIPTURE SPEAKS VOLUMES about the Christian Walk as a walk of love; about the Christian becoming a fragrant offering. To me, one phrase is especially laden with meaning "As poor, yet making many rich."

What a powerful paradox: The poor making many rich. There are many variations we could play on that theme, but here is the one let's settle on: Our ministry as Christians is that of making many rich. No matter the circumstances under which we live, whether we're rich or poor, whether we're young or old, whether we are educated or uneducated—no matter who we are as Christians, our ministry is the ministry of making many rich.

And here is the good news for every one of us. No matter where we are in life, no matter what is going on in our lives right now, no matter what our economic circumstances may be just now, we can still make many rich. But how do we do it? How do we make many rich?

First of all, we make many rich by sharing the good news of salvation. People are hungry to hear the good news of salvation from persons who are living witnesses of God's gracious redemption and transforming love. And, second, we can make many rich by letting them know by our love, care, and attention that they are important, that they mean something to God and to us.

That is the poverty of people. They do not believe they count. Nobody has ever told them or shown them that they do.

On Christmas Eve, 1988, a congregation of United Methodists in Nebraska had a wonderful opportunity to do that. Their pastor, Rev. Jean Samuelson, told how it all came about. Apparently a transient moved into the community who frightened many persons especially children. It had to do with his appearance. He was poorly dressed, smelled badly, and was usually drunk. He was also crippled and had a scarred and contorted face. People avoided him, but not Rev. Samuelson. She tried to visit with him and always invited him to attend church. If she saw him on the street or in a store, she would invite him, but he always declined. In time she managed to discover why he was so badly crippled. He had been stabbed many times by his father when he was a small boy!

During the Christmas Eve service, the man stumbled into the church, drunk. He found a seat in the back of the sanctuary. When Rev. Samuelson offered the invitation for persons to come forward for Communion, this man managed to get to his feet and waving a piece of paper in his hand cried out, "Stop Rev. Samuelson. I want you to read this poem." Jean Samuelson is a very kind and compassionate person. She knew that this man had been hurt many times in life, so in kindness she suggested that perhaps they go on with the service and she would read the poem later. That would not do. He cried out again, "Stop. I want you to read this poem." With that he began to come down the aisle. Because of his drunken condition, he tripped and fell, hitting and cutting his head on the end of one of the pews. It was then she noticed that not only was his head bleeding, but his hand and arm were also badly bleeding because he had fallen down on the step coming into the church.

She took the poem and tried to read it. She said it did not seem to make much sense. "Like the snow, I am falling, falling, falling. Like the night, I am falling, falling, falling." Then, she said, there were some lines that made no sense at all. Something about his dog. She was trying to think quickly on her feet. She knew she could not go on reading the poem. Yet something told her that she must.

She came to the end of the poem which went something like this: "Like the snow, falling, falling, falling. Like the night, falling, falling, falling, I think that I am falling, falling, falling in love with Jesus Christ." Rev. Samuelson said that a powerful silence fell over the church. People were deeply moved. Some of the people helped the man down to the communion rail. As the people knelt, tears of love, sorrow and joy streamed down their faces (Wilmoth, January 8, 1989).

A real miracle happened in that church on Christmas Eve. It was the miracle of a congregation coming to an awareness of who they were. It was the miracle of an awareness that the spirit of God was upon them to heal the brokenhearted, to proclaim release to the captives, to help the blind recover their sight, and to set free those who are bruised.

It was an awareness that we are called to make others rich by sharing the good news of salvation and by letting them know by our love, care, and attention that they are important, that they mean something to God.

Reflecting and Recording

Name three people you know who need to hear the good news of salvation.

_____   _____   _____

Name three people you know who need to know by love, care, and attention that they are important and that they mean something to God. Spend time in prayer about how you can make these persons rich.

_____   _____   _____

During the Day

Put into action what you concluded in your prayer.

DAY SEVEN
Christ's Love Perfected in Us

HERE IS AN AMAZING PHENOMENON: Through our love, Christ's love is perfected. That is what John said: "If we love one another, God abides in us and his love is perfected in us" (1 John 4:12).

Here is a letter from a young fellow who was just starting out in the ministry. He was about half-way through his second year of seminary. I have some reservations about sharing it. I know the young man was seeing me through rose-colored glasses. He hasn't experienced me stumbling and falling in my walk of love. But I share it for two reasons. First of all, to remind myself of what any person's ministry (lay and clergy) is all about. And second, to remind us all that the walk of love is possible for any one of us.

Dear Maxie:

Life is going pretty well, Maxie. I do not get much sleep, but what else is new? I still struggle with the call some and wonder if this is the place to be and the thing to be doing. People ask the questions that I do not know the answer to and my counseling load has gotten heavier. I find that I am my worst critic and struggle to keep ahead of mediocrity. I know my insecurities—they don't. I know my fears—they can't conceive them. I feel my weaknesses as this work takes the strength. Is it possible that I can make a difference—the difference? Should I be spending this time getting my feet on the ground before I offer gravity to another? Even in the struggle, life is going well. When it is difficult to go ahead, I tend to look back at what brought me here. Someone knew my name, hugged my neck and offered me their hand. In them I saw the Christ, and it is that Christ that I know brought me here. So here it is, Sir, and it is not Cyprian or Augustine, Luther or Wesley. It is the Christ in you, your face, hands and heart that helps me take that first step of the day. God bless you. I love you.

Amazingly, through our love, the love of Christ is perfected. And that love is always a fragrant offering.

Reflecting and Recording

On **DAY ONE** and **DAY TWO** of this week, you were asked to describe persons who have been special to you. Go back and read your notes about those persons and see what characteristics in their life you might cultivate in your own life to help it become a more fragrant offering.

During the Day

Continue putting your prayer of yesterday into practice.

If you are using this workbook with a group, make preparations for your meeting, and pray for those who are sharing with you.

WEEK SIX
Group Meeting

Introduction

You are drawing to the close of this adventure. This meeting and the next are the last planned group meetings. At this one, your group may want to discuss the future. Would they like to stay together for a longer time? Are there books, tapes, and so forth they would like to use corporately? If you're part of the same church, is there a way they might share the experience with others in the church?

Sharing Together

1. Begin with the leader opening with prayer or calling on someone else to do so (consult them ahead of time), then sing a chorus or hymn everyone knows.
2. Invite two or three persons to share their description of the one person they know who best personifies "a fragrant offering" (from **DAY ONE**).
3. Invite two or three persons to share the person who has been the primary *Yes* in their life (from **DAY TWO**).
4. Spend ten to fifteen minutes discussing the call of love to "hang tough." Urge the group members to share personal experiences.
5. Spend eight to ten minutes discussing the statement: "How we feel about money and how we use it tells the story of *who* and *whose* we are.
6. Invite as many as would like to share briefly an experience of making another person rich, either by sharing the good news of salvation, or by enabling them to know that they are important.

Praying Together

1. In the closing time of prayer, invite any who wish to do so to share a situation they face that calls for tough love. Invite one person to pray in response to the sharing, calling the people by name.
2. Now invite persons to share the names of persons outside the group that they know who are faced with similar situations.
3. Share these and other special requests, and then enter into a period of group prayer, with persons praying aloud as they wish for those needs mentioned.
4. Close your time of prayer with *The Lord's Prayer*.

Pictures

Select new pictures for prayer this coming week.

Singing in the Rain

DAY ONE

Walk of Joy

Truly, truly, I say to you, you will weep and lament, but the world will rejoice;
you will be sorrowful, but your sorrow will turn into joy.   —John 16:20

A CARTOON PICTURED A MAN IN A DOCTOR'S OFFICE receiving a physical examination. The doctor came out of his private office with a series of papers and a chart to give the patient the results of all the tests. These were the doctor's words: "Well, I see no reason why you can't live a perfectly normal life, as long as you don't try to enjoy it."

Then there is the story of a teenager who was overheard to say to a donkey out in the country, "Why, you must be a Christian, you have a long face like Grandpa."

All of that is to introduce the idea that the Christian Walk is a joyful walk. Let's forever be done with the notion of a mule-faced, pinch-faced, dark-clouded, droop-shouldered Christianity, whose adherents look as though they had been baptized in lemon juice.

Now I know that merely living doesn't always inspire us to employ our heart and soul and senses to express joy. It is not as easy as saying that behind every cloud is a silver lining.

In one of the "Peanuts" cartoons, Charles Schulz pictures Lucy at her psychiatric counseling center, offering her wisdom at the rate of 5 cents per session. Charlie Brown is there, and he says to her, "And I remember what you told me." He goes on to say, "You said that when I became depressed, I should always remember that every cloud has a silver lining." Then he produces his cloud and says, "I want you to look at this." He holds up a cloud that doesn't have a silver lining. Instead, it has a very, very dark lining.

Lucy takes it, and in her best doctor expression, she says, "Hmm . . . very interesting . . . I think I see the problem." Then she concludes, "What we have here is a defective cloud."

Well, it's that way a lot in many of our lives. Living life is not as easy as affirming that every cloud has a silver lining. It seems as though, more often than not, the clouds of our lives—are defective clouds. But, for the Christian, the source of joy is beyond merely living. It is a quality of life not dependent upon circumstances.

Some of you may be old enough to remember the movie *Singin' in the Rain*. Was it Gene Kelly or Fred Astaire who sang and danced his way through the entire show? The title alone has become a metaphor for poets, songwriters, and others to express triumph in the face of tragedy, joy in the face of oppressive circumstances.

There is a story in the Book of Acts that presents it clearly. It is the story of two preachers who learn to "sing in the rain." The rains of persecution were falling on the first century church. Christians were being seen as a threat and were being persecuted. Paul and Silas had been attacked by a mob. The judges, before whom they were taken by the mob, became so angry that they tore off Paul and Silas's clothes. That would hardly pass for proper courtroom decorum. They were beaten by the prison guards and thrown into the dungeon of the Philippian jail where their feet were secured in stocks. Yet, in that place and in those circumstances, they sang.

A strange place in which to sing, wouldn't you say? They also prayed. Now, that's not so surprising. Most of us pray when we get into trouble. We would have been surprised had Paul and Silas not prayed. But to sing, to be joyous and praise God, is something new, something remarkable in those circumstances.

This incident is one of the most triumphant notes in New Testament Christianity. It is an unforgettable illustration of what faith ought to do for us. It is faith's genius to sing in all sorts of difficult, even devastating, circumstances. It is easy enough to be happy in pleasant circumstances when life is sunny and bright and everything is moving along like a song. The person who cannot rejoice in the beauty of nature about him, in the gracious gift of life, when the sun is shining and he has health, home, work and friends, has to be the most insensitive and ungrateful of creatures. But to sing in a dungeon and at midnight—when happiness is a victory and cheerfulness a miracle—is a special gift and grace of the Christian's hope and faith in God (Thompson, p. 55).

So the Christian Walk is a walk of joy.

Now let me give you a banner word—a word to memorize and remember: "Joy is the banner flying high over the castle of my heart when the King is in residence there."

Now let me put that singing truth into a theological statement: Joy is the gift of the Spirit that becomes a condition of the heart which is confident of its relationship with Christ.

Reflecting and Recording

What has been your most joyful experience in the past three months? Locate it in your memory, trying to get in touch with it in your thoughts and feelings, and describe it without being bound by structure or complete sentences. Use a stream-of-conscious writing style, in whatever words or phrases capture it best.

During the Day

Try to be alive to things that may remind you of your joyful experience and continue to celebrate it throughout the day. Memorize this banner word and let it sing in your heart during the day:

Joy is the banner flying high over the castle of my heart
when the King is in residence there.

DAY TWO
The Joy of Salvation

Joy is the gift of the Spirit
that becomes a condition
of the heart which is
confident of its relationship with Christ.

THE NUMBER ONE REASON FOR THIS IS OUR SALVATION. C. S. Lewis entitled his autobiography *Surprised By Joy*. To be saved, to know the salvation of the Lord, is to be overtaken with joy. Any person who knows the peace that comes from the sense of sins forgiven, of reconciliation with God, and of relief from guilt is a person of joy.

Do you remember the three parables Jesus told about the lost and the found in Luke 15? This chapter has been called "the Gospel within the Gospel."

A woman lost a coin. She lit her lamp and swept the house diligently until she found it, and when she found it, she called her friends and neighbors together, saying to them, "Rejoice with me, for I have found the coin which I had lost." And Jesus adds to that, "Even so, I tell you, there is joy before the angels of God over one sinner who repents."

Then there is the story of the lost sheep. A shepherd was willing to leave his ninety-nine in the wilderness, and to go after the one which was lost until he finds it. And when he finds it, he lays it on his shoulders, and he carries it home, rejoicing. And when he arrives, he calls together his friends and neighbors, saying to them, "Rejoice with me, for I have found my sheep which was lost."

Again, the word of Jesus is, "Even so, I tell you, there will be more joy in heaven over one sinner who repents than over ninety-nine righteous persons who need no repentance."

Of course, the last of those three parables of the lost and the found is that of the lost son, and how well we know that story. But sense again the celebration when the son had finally come home, when the one who was dead to the father was now alive again, when the one who was lost was found.

"Bring the best robe and put it on him; and put a ring on his hand, and shoes on his feet; and bring the fatted calf and kill it, and let us eat and make merry."

What rejoicing! To be saved is to be overtaken with joy.

There is a story making the rounds about the man who wandered into the back room of a tavern. He was amazed to see a large dog playing poker with five men. He walked up to a gentlemen who was observing the action and said: "My goodness, that dog is fantastic. I've never seen anything like it."

"I don't think he's so great," came the laconic reply. "Every time he gets a good hand he starts wagging his tail."

Am I being irreverent when I say we've been dealt an unbeatable hand? No wonder we "wag our tails"—we've been given salvation. That is the source of our joy.

Reflecting and Recording

One of the weaknesses of the present-day church is that we do not have many settings in which to tell our own "story." If you are sharing this workbook with a group, you have such a setting, and you have been telling each other your stories.

So much negative "stuff" has surrounded the notion of Christian witnessing—the stereotypical "brother-are-you-saved" and countless variations on that theme—that we mainline Christians have left witnessing to others. That is a tragedy. Witnessing is simply storytelling. And if we are Christians, we all have a salvation story to tell.

Make some notes that would be an outline for you in telling your story, and include especially some expression of "the joy of salvation."

During the Day

If you haven't memorized the banner word as I suggested yesterday, work on it some more, and sing it in your heart. Look for a chance today to tell your "Joy of Salvation" story.

DAY THREE

The Joy of Fellowship with Christ

If you abide in me, and my words abide in you, ask whatever you will, and it shall be done for you. By this my Father is glorified, that you bear much fruit, and so prove to be my disciples. As the Father has loved me, so have I loved you; abide in my love. If you keep my commandments, you will abide in my love, just as I have kept my Father's commandments and abide in his love. These things I have spoken to you, that my joy may be in you, and that your joy may be full.
                                                              —John 15:7 -11

ANY PERSON WHO KNOWS THE PEACE that comes from the sense of sins forgiven, of reconciliation with God, and of relief from guilt is a person of joy. But there is another primary source of joy: fellowship with Christ.

We could talk about that in a lot of different ways. There is prayer, our personal and private devotional life. And there is our corporate worship with songs and music of praise. We could talk about sharing with other Christians in study and fellowship. Of course, there is the Eucharist, the Holy Communion, where the Lord welcomes us to his table to dine with him. What a beautiful image that is—gathering at the Lord's table with the Lord himself as our host.

It is not normal that you would have a theology of the Eucharist in the old gospel songs sung in country Baptist churches. That is usually the task of the Roman Catholic, Episcopal, or Methodist composers like Charles Wesley. But we had such a hymn at the Eastside Baptist Church down in Perry County, Mississippi. We didn't really associate it with Eucharist, or the Last Supper, as we called it when we celebrated it, which was generally twice a year at the most. But it was a Eucharist hymn, pure and simple.

> Jesus has a table spread
> Where the saints of God are fed
> He invites His chosen people, "Come and dine;"
> With His manna He doth feed
> And supplies our every need;
> O 'tis sweet to sup with Jesus all the time!

And how the chorus would ring out:

> "Come and dine," the Master calleth,
> "Come and dine;"
> You may feast at Jesus' table all the time;
> He who fed the multitude,
> Turned the water into wine,
> To the hungry calleth now, "Come and dine."

For those weary, tired, hardworking, suffering, poverty-bound folks, it was the very best image for fellowship—a meal together.

You see, joy of fellowship with Christ comes through prayer, through corporate worship, through music and praise, and through the holy meal where the Lord welcomes us to his table to dine with him.

But, fellowship with Christ also comes through serving his children. Mother Teresa talks about that kind of fellowship in terms of joy as well.

> Joy is strength; joy is love; joy is a net of love by which you can catch souls. . . . She gives most who gives with joy. The best way to show our gratitude to God and the people is to accept everything with joy. A joyful heart is the inevitable result of a heart burning with love. . . .
>
> We all long for heaven where God is, but we have it in our power to be in heaven with him right now—to be happy with him at this very moment. But being happy with him now means:
> loving as he loves,
> helping as he helps,
> giving as he gives,
> serving as he serves,
> rescuing as he rescues,
> being with him for all the twenty-four hours,
> touching him in his distressing disguise (Mother Teresa, pp. 77-78).

I hear it all the time from people involved in serving ministries. "I feel Christ's presence when I deliver those Meals on Wheels." "You knew that Christ was there at the day shelter for the homeless." "I know I didn't have to go to Costa Rica to experience Christ—but he was more real to me than ever before in those poverty-bound children that we had in our Bible school."

Fellowship with Christ comes through serving his children.

Reflecting and Recording

On a scale of 1 to 10, with 10 being the highest, rate the following channels in terms of the joy you receive from fellowship with Christ

    ( ) Personal Prayer
    ( ) Group Bible Study
    ( ) Daily Devotions
    ( ) Prayer Group
    ( ) Corporate Worship
    ( ) Personal Witnessing
    ( ) Holy Communion
    ( ) Serving others for Christ's sake

Reflect on your responses. Are you missing a good bit of joy?

***

During the Day

There are at least two of the above channels, personal witnessing and serving others in Christ's name, that you can yet do if you are beginning your day. If you are closing it, you can do them tomorrow. Give it a try.

DAY FOUR

The Circumstances of Life
Do Not Condition Our Joy But Confirm It

I am the vine, you are the branches. He who abides in me, and I in him, he it is that bears much fruit, for apart from me you can do nothing. If a man does not abide in me, he is cast forth as a branch and withers; and the branches are gathered, thrown into the fire and burned. If you abide in me, and my words abide in you, ask whatever you will, and it shall be done for you. By this my Father is glorified, that you bear much fruit, and so prove to be my disciples. As the Father has loved me, so have I loved you; abide in my love. If you keep my commandments, you will abide in my love, just as I have kept my Father's commandments and abide in his love. These things I have spoken to you, that my joy may be in you, and that your joy may be full.   —John 15:5-11

> Truly, truly, I say to you, you weep and lament, but the world will rejoice; you will be sorrowful, but your sorrow will turn into joy. When a woman is in travail she has sorrow, because her hour has come; but when she is delivered of the child, she no longer remembers the anguish, for joy that a child is born into the world. So you have sorrow now, but I will see you again and your hearts will rejoice, and no one will take your joy from you. —John 16:20-22

JOY IS THE GIFT OF THE SPIRIT that becomes a condition of the heart which is confident of its relationship with Christ. That is the essence of joy.

So, we need to keep reminding ourselves that joy is more than pleasure, more than happiness. It is a blessedness that is ours because we are fulfilled in our relationship with Christ, and that relationship with Christ is bringing fulfillment in every area of our life. The circumstances of our life do not condition our joy, but confirm it. That means that even in the depths of the night, God is present with us, and we can know joy.

On **DAY ONE** of this week, I told the story of Paul and Silas, as recorded in the Book of Acts. In that story, Luke makes a special point that it was at midnight that Paul and Silas broke into singing. So singing at midnight is a symbol of the radical dimension of Christian hope and Christian joy. Singing in the rain, singing at midnight!

Did you note the contexts in which Jesus speaks of joy in the scriptures above? In the first one, he is talking about love and about keeping the commandments, and he says, "If you do this—if you keep my commandments and abide in my love, you will know joy." But in the second one, he speaks of joy in the midnight hour, of joy that brings about singing in the rain. He says that we will weep and lament and that we will be sorrowful, but our sorrow will turn to joy.

In the depths of the night, God is present and we can know joy. Leslie Weatherhead tells this story:

> Some time ago I had the privilege of meeting and speaking with Hugh Redwood. He said that on one occasion, at a time when he was under severe nervous strain, not knowing which way to turn concerning certain decisions he had to make, he was staying at a friend's house prior to speaking at a big meeting. His friend said to him, "You look tired. Would you like to escape all this chatter, and rest in a room upstairs?" Mr. Redwood said that he would like it more than anything else, and to his delight, a bright fire was burning, an easy chair was drawn up near it, and at his elbow there was a little table with an open Bible upon it. The Bible was open at Ps. 59 and in the margin opposite

verse 10 someone had written in pencil an interpretation which kindled his mind as it does my own. In the Bible we read, "The God of my mercy shall prevent me," where, of course, the word "prevent" means "go before." But the penciled interpretation ran thus: "My God in his loving kindness *shall meet me at every corner.*" Mr. Redwood said that it came to him as light in a dark place, light from the very heart of God. It cheered him immensely. He made his decision. He turned his corner successfully (Weatherhead, p. 115).

Remember: The circumstances of life do not condition our joy but confirm it.

Reflecting and Recording

In your reflection, get in touch with some tough, up-against-it experience in which you knew joy, because God was with you. Make some notes about that experience—when it was, what it was, who was involved, what you were risking and feeling, and the outcome of it.

During the Day

Work on what I asked you to do yesterday. Experience joy, either by personal witnessing or serving another for Christ's sake.

DAY FIVE

"The Little Madness of Hope"

Blessed be the God and Father of our Lord Jesus Christ! By his great mercy we have been born anew to a living hope through the resurrection of Jesus Christ from the dead, and to an inheritance which is imperishable, undefiled, and unfading, kept in heaven for you, who by God's power are guarded through faith for a salvation ready to be revealed in the last time. In this you rejoice, though now for a little while you may have to suffer various trials, so that the genuineness of your faith, more precious than gold which though perishable is tested by fire, may redound to praise and glory and honor at the revelation of Jesus Christ. Without having seen him you love him; though you do not now see him you believe in him and rejoice with unutterable and exalted joy. As the outcome of your faith you obtain the salvation of your souls.   —1 Peter 1:3-9

WE HAVE BEEN TALKING ABOUT JOY. Akin to joy is hope, and hope gives us the energy for our Christian Walk.

Zorba is one of my favorite movie and stage productions. The theatre experience was especially memorable for me when Anthony Quinn played Zorba. The climax of the drama is two men—Zorba and his boss—dancing. The boss's money is invested in an untried invention to bring timber down a mountain. The wood is badly needed by the community, and it is to be used to reinforce the walls of an old mine which, it is hoped, will restore economic life to the village. Everyone turned out to watch the great occasion. Anticipation turned quickly to gloom as the weight of the logs caused the unproven slide to collapse. The dejected man, whose money was lost, pondered leaving the village. But the words of Zorba get his attention: "I like you too much not to say it, you've got everything, except one thing—madness. A man needs a little madness or else . . . he never dares cut the rope and be free."

Then standing before the dismal pile of rubble, Zorba begins to laugh, and says, "Hey Boss, did you ever see a more splendiferous crash?"

With renewed perspective, the boss asks, "Teach me to dance, will you?" The story closes with the two dancing and celebrating life at the sight of their greatest failure.

At the heart of the Christian faith is Easter, and Easter is about the little madness to be free to dance and celebrate because there has been a resurrection. The stupendous crash that took place on Golgotha, the huge stone shouting no to life as it was placed over the cave tomb in which Jesus' body was laid—that crash is swallowed up in laughing and alleluias and shouting and dancing.

Peter summarized the meaning of our Easter faith: "Blessed be the God and Father of our Lord Jesus Christ! By his great mercy we have been born anew to a living hope through the resurrection of Jesus Christ from the dead."

Each of the Gospels tells the Easter story slightly differently. But in each telling, there is the suggestion of more than just a little madness of hope. Luke tells of the women going to the tomb early on Sunday morning, taking spices to anoint Jesus' body. But when they go into the tomb, they cannot find the body. Two men in dazzling apparel frighten them as one of them says, "Why do you seek the living among the dead?" Then he reminds them of how Jesus Christ had told them that he would be delivered into the hands of sinful men and be crucified and, on the third day, rise. It is then that they remember, and they return to the eleven disciples to share the great good news.

The result: "But these words seemed to them an idle tale, and they did not believe them" (Luke 24:11). A little madness there.

In each of the Gospels it's the same. In Mark's Gospel, the women who see Jesus on Easter morning "said nothing to anyone, for they were afraid." A little madness. In Matthew's Gospel, the authorities tell the guards they must "tell people his disciples came by night and stole him away while we were asleep." A little madness. In John's Gospel, the disciples lock themselves in a room, in fear and despair. A little madness.

But the madness changes. Something is added when the fact of the resurrection dawns fully upon them. Hope is added, and with it, the little madness of hope.

Elmer Homrighausen, one-time teacher and dean at Princeton Theological Seminary calls hope "the oxygen of the soul."

Much emphasis is today being placed upon the unique and creative power of imagination. While fantasizing and day dreaming and imagining do have dangers because they may dissociate persons from hard realities, they are nevertheless great capacities without which human beings become matter-of-factish flatlanders.

Without hope the person soon becomes prosaic and pedestrian. He or she loses the will to rise above enslaving conditions and envision a brighter future. Hope is the oxygen of the soul. Without it one suffocates, and hope deferred makes the heart sick (Homrighausen, p. 26).

Christians have a unique perspective on hope. The risen Christ gives substance to our hope.

In his eyes, the doctor revealed to Joseph that death was close by. His Aunt May and Grandma and Grandpa gave him anything he wanted. "I had dreams. I had hopes. I had ambitions—but I was running out of hope." On his 9th birthday, there was the usual ice cream, cake, candles, balloons, and books— all things for a bed-ridden child. But then Uncle Bob came on the scene. Uncle Bob, the no- good scoundrel uncle who always smelled of gin.

"Where's my birthday-boy? Where's my Buddy?" he said, brushing by Grandma as she ate her cake. Uncle Bob sat next to Joseph on the canvas bed and shoved a box into his face, saying, "Happy Birthday!"

Opening it, Joseph began to cry. Grandpa moved toward Bob with incredible speed. "How silly! How insensitive!" shouted Grandpa as Joseph cried all the more. Then Joseph held up a pair of ball-bearing roller skates—the only gift he received for when he would get well. Someone believed he would live (Pool, May 3, 1987).

For Joseph, Uncle Bob gave substance to his hope in those ball-bearing roller skates. Everybody else had accepted the prognosis—that Joseph was going to die of tuberculosis. But it was those ball-bearing skates that gave him the hope. He lived to be a man telling the story himself.

And that is what Paul was saying in our text: "Blessed be the God and Father of our Lord Jesus Christ! By his great mercy we have been born anew to a living hope through the resurrection of Jesus Christ from the dead."

Reflecting and Recording

Consider the claim that hope is the energy for our Christian Walk. Has it been so for you?

***

Recall an experience when only hope kept you going. Record that experience here.

Do you know someone who is up against it, for whom hope is the energy keeping them going? Close your time of reflection in prayer for that person.

During the Day

Give the person you just prayed for a telephone call or write a note of encouragement.

DAY SIX
The Energy of Hope

On the evening of that day, the first day of the week, the doors being shut where the disciples were, for fear of the Jews, Jesus came and stood among them and said to them, "Peace be with you." When he had said this, he showed them his hands and his side. Then the disciples were glad when they saw the Lord. Jesus said to them again, "Peace be with you. As the Father has sent me, even so I send you." And when he had said this, he breathed on them, and said to them, "Receive the Holy Spirit.
                                                                    —John 20:19-22

THE DISCIPLES ARE ALL HERE IN THE UPPER ROOM, EXCEPT THOMAS. Though the doors are shut and locked because of their fear, Jesus appears. He shows them his wounds to prove he is not a ghost. Then he breathes on them.

That is the way God did it at creation. He breathed life into Adam and Eve. What is happening here is something new being created. This is John's way of telling of the birth of the Church. Luke, in the Book of Acts, says that on Pentecost, God breathed the Holy Spirit upon Jesus' followers. Both stories say the same thing: the Spirit is breathed upon the people and the Church is born. The Spirit is the spirit of Jesus, the resurrected Christ.

The Holy Spirit, the spirit of Jesus as the resurrected Christ, is the *energy* of hope. And we can walk in hope as Christians because we know that *Christ can do for us what we can't do for ourselves.*

Go back to John's story of Easter. The disciples had locked themselves up but Christ entered anyway. That is a powerful image. Christ is not stopped by our doors of fear or weakness or guilt or despair. He does for us what we are unable to do for ourselves.

So you have trouble in your marriage. You are not even willing to talk about it. Christ will enter the situation anyway, if you are willing. You are fearful for your job security and haven't told anyone about it. Christ will enter your workplace when you are open to him. So you are in a period of family crisis, Christ will enter.

We all have unanswered questions and that is okay. Christ will enter anyway. What happened to the disciples is no isolated incident. Christ moves through whatever walls we build or doors we close or shades we draw. Christ does for us what we are unable to do for ourselves.

Then, there is a second reason that we can walk in hope. Christ does for us what others can't do for us.

Do you remember John Irving's novel *The Hotel New Hampshire?* In the novel, John's sister Franny is raped. The family seeks to help her in her physical suffering, but she locks herself in a bathroom. John calls to her through the bathroom door, asking if there was anything he could get for her.

"Thank you," she whispered. "Just go out and get me yesterday and most of today," she said. "I want them back."

Well, John couldn't do that for Franny. But Jesus can.

Oh, he can't give us back our yesterday, he can do better than that. He can forgive the sins of yesterday. He can heal the pain of yesterday. He can restore the energy wasted in the selfish pursuits of yesterday. He can restore the relationships that, in our sin and selfishness and pride, we severed yesterday.

You see, Christ does for us not only what we can't do for ourselves, but also what others can't do for us.

So the resurrection of Christ gives substance to our hope. Hope is the energy of our Christian Walk.

Reflecting and Recording

Spend a few minutes calling to mind, and thanking God for, those times when Christ did for you what you nor others could never have done.

***

During the Day

Copy this verse and take it with you to use during flash prayer times.

> Blessed be the God and Father of our Lord Jesus Christ! By his great mercy we have been born anew to a living hope through the resurrection of Jesus Christ from the dead.
> — Peter 1:3

DAY SEVEN

Tomorrow Is Going to Be All Right

THOUGH EVERYTHING IS NOT GOING TO BE ALL RIGHT TOMORROW, tomorrow is going to be all right.

Now, that's not double-talk. Peter expressed it this way:

> In this you rejoice, though now for a little while you may have to suffer various trials, so that the genuineness of your faith, more precious than gold which though perishable is tested by fire, may redound to praise and glory and honor at the revelation of Jesus Christ. Without having seen him you love him; though you do not now see him you believe in him and rejoice with unutterable and exalted joy.
> —1 Peter 1:6-8

Do you see it? Everything may not be all right tomorrow, but tomorrow will be all right, because Jesus will be with us tomorrow.

One of my spiritual advisors and prayer partners is now-retired Bishop Lance Webb. He and his wife Elizabeth became dear friends of ours fifteen years ago.

Elizabeth died in March, 1990. She and Lance had a marvelous life together, did almost everything together, and shared a common faith that continued to grow even well into their seventies.

They had been to Hawaii on a vacation. While there, Elizabeth became a bit ill. When they returned, she went into the hospital. They soon learned it was serious. There was a series of aneurysms that could not be repaired; the fiber was too thin. Yet, surgery was required.

They were together the morning before the surgery. They read some psalms and prayed together that night after surgery, and Lance went home. As he was leaving, Elizabeth said, "I will see you in the morning, or I will be with the angels." Well, she's with the angels. She died that night. What a glorious way to go.

Everything may not be all right tomorrow, but tomorrow will be all right, because Jesus will be with us. He will be with us to do for us what we can't do for ourselves, and to do what others can't do for us. And in all the tomorrows it will be that way.

Hope is the energy of the Christian Walk, and the living Christ is the substance of that hope.

Reflecting and Recording

Look back over the seven weeks of this workbook experience. Think about what you have learned, the questions raised, the new ideas, what you disagreed with, the challenges to change, the promises of hope. Using single words or short phrases, write down what the experience has meant to you.

-

During the Day, and all the days ahead—
walk in newness of life;
walk in Christ.

WEEK SEVEN
Group Meeting

Introduction

This is the last meeting designed for this group. You may have already talked about the possibility of continuing to meet. You should conclude those plans. Some groups find it meaningful to select two or three weeks of the workbook and go through those weeks again as an extension of their time together. Others continue for an additional set time, using other resources. Whatever you choose to do, it is usually helpful to determine the actual time line so that persons can make a clear commitment.

Another possibility that has been very effective in our congregation in Memphis is for one or two persons to decide they will recruit and lead a group of new persons through this workbook. Many people are looking for a small group growth experience, and this is a way to respond to that need.

Sharing Together

1. Begin your sharing time by singing the chorus "Down in my heart" or another familiar chorus of praise.
2. Invite two or three persons to share their most joyful experience of the past three months. When those persons have shared, discuss as a group what God had to do with the experiences.
3. Spend ten to fifteen minutes discussing this statement: Joy is the gift of the Spirit that becomes a condition of the heart which is confident of its relationship with Christ.
4. Invite two or three to tell their "joy of salvation story" (from **DAY TWO**).
5. Invite two or three persons to share an experience in which they knew joy even though they were suffering or up against it (from **DAY FOUR**).
6. Spend six to eight minutes discussing the claim that "Hope is the energy of our Christian Walk."
7. Invite two or three persons to share an experience of Christ doing something for them which they nor others could do.

Praying Together

1. Begin your time of prayer by asking each person to express gratitude to God in a two or three sentence prayer for something significant that has happened to him or her as a result of these seven weeks.

2. Give each person the opportunity to share whatever decision or commitment he or she has made, or will make, concerning the Christian Walk. It is important that these be specific. Follow each person's verbalizing of these decisions and commitments by having another person in the group offer a brief prayer of thanksgiving and support for that person.

3. A benediction is a blessing or greeting shared with another, or by a group, in parting. The "passing of the peace" is such a benediction. You take a person's hand, look into his or her eyes, and say, "The peace of the Lord be with you," and the person responds, "And may the Lord's peace be yours." Then that person, taking the hands of the person next to him or her, says "The peace of the Lord be with you," and receives the response, "And may the Lord's peace be yours." Standing in a circle, let the leader "pass the peace," and let it go around the circle.

4. Having completed the passing of the peace, speak to one another in a more spontaneous way. Move about to different persons in the group, saying whatever you feel is appropriate for your parting blessing to each person. Or you may simply embrace the person and say nothing. In your own unique way, "bless" each person who has shared this journey with you.

Notes & Bibliography

Sources quoted in this workbook are identified by author and page number. Bibliographic information for each source is listed below.

Brokhoff, Barbara. "God's Pass/Fail Exam" in *Pulpit Digest,* September-October, 1982.

Davidson, J.A. "Christian: Noun or Adjective" in *Pulpit Digest,* July-August, 1983.

Eisley, Loren. *All The Strange Hours.* New York: Charles Scribner's Sons, 1975.

Faulkner, William. *The Sound & the Fury.* New York: Random House, 1954.

Fosdick, Harry Emerson. *The Living of These Days: an Autobiography.* New York: Harper & Brothers, 1956.

Goodspeed, Edgar J. *The Meaning of Ephesians.* Chicago: University of Chicago Press, 1933.

Homrighausen, Elmer G. "Oxygen of the Soul" in *Pulpit Digest,* January-February, 1979.

Kalas, Ellsworth J. "Star Performer" (unpublished sermon) August 18, 1985.

Lewis, C.S. *The Weight of Glory.* Grand Rapids, MI: William B. Eerdmans Publishing Company, 1949.

Littel, Franklin H., ed. *Sermons to Intellectuals.* New York: The MacMillan Company, 1963.

MacKay, John A. *God's Order.* New York: The MacMillan Company, 1953.

McAllaster, Elva. *Free to be Single.* Chappaqua, NY: Christian Herald Books, 1979.

McDonald, George. *The Princess and The Goblin.* New York: Puffin Books, 1984.

Moore, Jim. "We're Not Alone" (unpublished sermon) July 9, 1989.

Mother Teresa. *A Gift for God.* New York: Harper & Row Publishers, Inc., 1975.

Muggeridge, Malcolm. *Something Beautiful for God.* London: William Collins Sons & Co Ltd, 1971.

Peterson, Eugene H. *A Long Obedience in the Same Direction.* Downers Grove, IL: InterVarsity Press, 1980.

Poole, Joe C. "Prisoners of Hope" (unpublished sermon) May 3, 1987.

Schwein, William M. "Who Is Responsible for that Empty Chair?" (unpublished sermon) January 11, 1987.

Shelby, Donald. "Healthy Conflict" (unpublished sermon) September 27, 1987.

Sumner, David E. "Saying Yes to Forgiveness" in *Pulpit Digest,* November-December, 1978.

Thompson, John. "Singing in the Rain" in *Pulpit Digest,* March-April, 1979.

Trotter, Mark. "You're Better Than You Think" (unpublished sermon) February 21, 1988.

Weatherhead, Leslie D. *Prescription for Anxiety.* Nashville, TN: Abingdon Press, 1979.

Wesley, John. *Works,* vol 1& 2. London: The Epworth Press, 1938.

Wilmoth, Rodney E. "From Declaration to Demonstration" (unpublished sermon) January 8, 1989.

About the Author

World Editor of The Upper Room from 1975 to 1982, Dr. Dunnam has been Senior Pastor of Christ United Methodist Church in Memphis, Tennessee since 1982. Prior to his being named World Editor, Dr. Dunnam was Director of Prayer Life and Fellowship of The Upper Room. He has served local pastorates in Georgia, Mississippi, and California. Dr. Dunnam is widely known as an evangelism leader and a pioneer in small group ministries.

Other books by Maxie Dunnam include *Channels of Challenge, Direction and Destiny, The Manipulator and the Church, Be Your Whole Self, Homesick for a Future, Dancing at My Funeral, A Way of Praying, Alive in Christ, The Communicator's Commentary, Our Journey: A Wesleyan View of the Christian Way,* and *Jesus' Claims—Our Promises.*

Dr. Dunnam holds the B.S. degree from the University of South Mississippi, the M.Th. degree from Emory University, and the D.D. degree from Asbury Theological Seminary.

The Workbook on the Christian Walk is the sixth book in Dr. Dunnam's popular workbook series.